CONCEIVING the HEAVENS

Creating the Science Fiction Novel

Melissa Scott

HEINEMANN
PORTSMOUTH, NH

Heinemann
A division of Reed Elsevier Inc.
361 Hanover Street
Portsmouth, NH 03801-3912
Offices and agents throughout the world

Library of Congress Cataloging-in-Publication Data
Scott, Melissa.
Conceiving the heavens : creating the science fiction novel /
Melissa Scott.
p. cm.
ISBN 0-435-07008-8
1. Science fiction—Authorship. I. Title.
PN3377.5.S3S37 1997
808.3'8762—dc21
97-24376
CIP

Editor: Cheryl Kimball
Production: Melissa L. Inglis
Cover design: Jenny Jensen Greenleaf
Manufacturing: Louise Richardson

Printed in the United States of America on acid-free paper
01 00 99 98 97 DA 1 2 3 4 5 6 7 8 9

CONTENTS

INTRODUCTION

A BRIEF DEFENSE OF SCIENCE FICTION, OR WHY DOES SOMEONE WHO WENT TO HARVARD WRITE THIS STUFF ANYWAY?

THIS IS A TRUE STORY. SHORTLY AFTER MY FIRST NOVEL WAS published, I went home to Arkansas to visit my family. I was flushed with pride: this 350-page paperback, with an astonishingly appropriate and attractive wrap-around cover, was entirely mine. The book was good enough to sell—only my second finished manuscript—and a few people outside my immediate circle of friends had said they liked it. It had even garnered a largely positive review in *Locus*, the major review organ for science fiction readers. So, as I say, I was quite pleased with myself, and, within the confines of the family where bragging is permitted, I said so. My parents seemed pleased for me as well, but there was a note of constraint in their praise that I couldn't quite identify. Then I helped my mother host one of their regular cocktail parties, at which my book was left prominently on the coffee table. Sure enough, one of my mother's more intellectually conservative friends picked it up, studied it, and looked quizzically at me.

"You wrote this," she said.

"Yes." I was beaming with pride, but she was oblivious, looking again at the cover with its spaceships and Roman arches.

"So tell me, Melissa," she said, "why does someone who went to Harvard write this stuff anyway?"

I was, needless to say, brought down sharply. I didn't know what to say: in the sheer pleasure of writing the manuscript, and then, beyond all expectation, having someone pay me to publish it, it had never occurred to me that I would need to justify my choice of subject. I finally stammered something feeble about "wanting to write what I liked to read," which got me through that party, but it's a question that has nagged at me ever since. Sure, I like to read science fiction, and it's absolutely true that there's no point in writing in any format that you yourself do not enjoy, but that answer begs the real question: why read—or write—science fiction?

Science fiction—SF to its friends—has a questionable reputation among more literary readers. It is unabashedly a genre fiction, but unlike mysteries or historical novels, there is no subset of science fiction that is generally acknowledged to be "literature." Science fiction's representatives on the best-seller lists tend to be novelizations of movies or series television rather than stand-alone novels that have reached a larger-than-genre audience. SF in fact seems to provoke only passionate responses. A librarian friend of mine (also an award-winning SF writer) has been given the job of teaching other librarians who don't like SF how to serve their readers who *do*. He usually begins his talk by comparing SF to black olives. Some people love them, he says, and some people hate them; this has nothing to do with the intrinsic merit of black olives, but everything to do with the individual's reaction to their taste. Science fiction, too, seems to be an unusual literary flavor. (The first thing most people say to me after finding out what I do for a living is "Oh, I never could get into science fiction." There's often a note of pride in their voices that I find more than a little disconcerting.) Academic criticism of science fiction, in itself a fairly recent phenomenon, has tended to focus on cyberpunk and feminist writing, and to take a postmodern, postliterary approach that removes the work studied from both genre and literary considerations.

I'm not really sure what produces this response—after all, I like SF (and black olives, for that matter)—and I'm not sure that the negative reasons are all that important. Most of the ones I've been given—things like clumsy writing, uninteresting characterization, overfamiliar plots—occur in other genres as well, without being assumed to be intrinsic to that genre. Instead, I think it's more useful to look at the positive reasons for reading and writing science fiction: what is it that I get from SF that I can't find in any other form?

The answer to that is very simple. Science fiction is the only genre that is predicated on the assumption of inevitable change. The point of both mystery and horror is to disrupt and then restore the status quo; historical novels reach back to an unchangeable past. The object of romance is to establish the heroine in the appropriate relationship, according to contemporary society, for a woman of her status; the Western posits a fixed set of (traditionally) masculine virtues and shows the rewards and perils of following that code. Science fiction, on the other hand, begins with the question, "What would happen if something was different from the way it is now?" The story, whatever it is, springs from that basic assumption of difference. Even the most fundamentally conservative works—the ones whose premises can be summed up as "everything is pretty much the way it is now, only with better toys and I'm in charge"— involve a significant change both to get the better toys and to put the writer's alter ego in control of this universe.

A lot of people find change uncomfortable. A genre based on exploring change seems to be a violation of the basic contract of genre writing, which is that this is not serious literature—genres are for leisure reading, escape, reassurance, not for confronting unpleasant possibilities. Science fiction, on the other hand, seems to revel in exploring potentially threatening changes: what if there were human beings who became gendered only on a monthly basis (Ursula K. Le Guin's *The Left Hand of Darkness*)? What if the very best drug in the galaxy could be produced only by torturing an intelligent but nonhuman species (*Brightness Falls from the Air* by James Tiptree Jr.)? What if the very structure of a language could be turned into a weapon that strikes its speakers (Samuel R. Delany's *Babel-17*)? What if the most violently antifeminist men ruled the world, and carried their beliefs about women—and men—to their logical extreme (Suzy McKee Charnas's *Walk to the End of the World*)? What if a mutation caused there to be five human sexes, but you lived on a world that acknowledged only two of them (my own *Shadow Man*)? It's no wonder that some people decline to face these kinds of challenges in their recreational reading—after all, we're all dealing with smaller versions of these same problems every day. People who like science fiction, on the other hand, find pleasure, escape, and even solace in reading these fictional exaggerations and expansions of contemporary questions.

This is not to say that science fiction people are necessarily more comfortable with change and the speed of change in the real world than are non-SF people. Some are, of course, just as there are some mystery readers whose real pleasure comes not from the restoration of the status quo, but from the exploration of its legitimacy before it is restored. Other SF readers are, if anything, hypersensitive to the changes around them, and find it easier to contemplate those changes when they are placed in a fictional and futuristic setting— divorced from immediate political or social consequence, or simply from contemporary buzzwords and emotional triggers. For some, science fiction is a safe place in which to confront ideas that upset, frighten, or attract them; for others, it's a way of imagining an otherwise intransigent and uncontrollable world remade to their specifications.

So why, exactly, does this someone who went to Harvard write science fiction? I don't make any claim to being more comfortable with change than most people (I probably fall into the hypersensitive category, if truth be told), but I do tend to assume its inevitability. Given that assumption, science fiction is the only form of literature that allows—indeed, requires—a writer to explore possible changes and their consequences. I want to tell stories, and I've discovered that the stories I want to tell are primarily ones that begin with "what might happen if." Science fiction is structured to tell an admittedly unreal story using all the techniques of realistic fiction, and the collision of the real and the unreal is what continues to draw me to this genre.

Science fiction functions on both an abstract, analytical level and a complex, emotional level, and lets me as a writer indulge in two things that I love: the imaginative reordering of our own world and the fictional working out of the consequences of those choices. Science fiction is, at its core, about the present rather than the future—a present seen through a distorting lens or in a curved mirror, exaggerating certain characteristics and hiding others, so that the writer presents a plausible "future" that still has something to say about the contemporary world. Or, to boil things down to the basics, science fiction lets a writer consider very abstract ideas in human, messy, and concrete terms. That's why I write science fiction.

PART

I

WRITING AS CRAFT

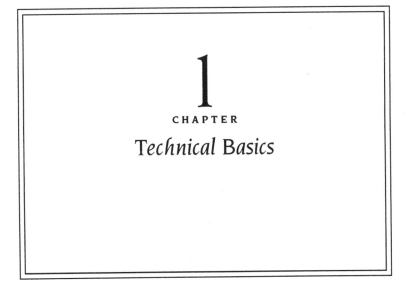

1

CHAPTER

Technical Basics

DESPITE WHAT SOME PEOPLE WILL TRY TO TELL YOU, WRITING science fiction is not an excuse to ignore the basics of good writing. In fact, SF requires a solid base of craft on which to build the extrapolations that are the heart of the field. Without that foundation, even the most exciting idea will fail to become a story. Yes, there are a few—a *very* few—exceptions to this rule, but in those cases some part of the story (not just the idea) had a spark of genius that allowed editor and readers to overlook the badly handled parts. As the field has matured, these exceptional cases have become few and far between. Fewer and fewer readers are willing to put up with bad writing for the sake of a good idea when there are so many good writers with equally good ideas working today. In general, it's easier to sweat the basics than to rely on a flash of pure genius to make your books worth reading.

So what are these basics? At bottom, you need to be able to do one simple thing: communicate your ideas in prose. The corollary to this is that you need to be comfortable with the standard form of your chosen language. This does not mean that you need to memorize the entire *Elements of Style* closely followed by the *Elements of Grammar* (though if you haven't got them memorized, you should probably own both of them). What it does mean is that the way in which you present your story should not get in the way of the story itself—and nothing destroys a reader's understanding more than misplaced commas, subject/verb disagreements, mangled possessives, and all the other possible deviations from the standard. Yes, it is possible to deviate from standard English in a narrative—to write in a real or invented dialect, to load the page with imagined futuristic slang, even to redefine the meaning of personal pronouns—but you have to do it extremely well to make it worth the effort your audience has to make to decipher your story.

The other basics of fiction are generally held to be plot, characterization, and setting, and writers are not exempt from providing them merely because they're working in a genre. One way of looking at this (I'm indebted to H. R. F. Keating's *On Writing Crime Fiction* for this idea) is to treat these obligations not as rules but as a *contract* between reader and writer. In presenting a manuscript as fiction, you have created—and agreed to fulfill—certain expectations on the part of your readers. In terms of plot, you've agreed to tell a story, something with a beginning, a middle, and an end. (Even if that end is three books down the line, it is implied—and if you don't deliver, your readers will be angry.) You've agreed to tell it fairly: any "surprise" endings must be set up, and you can't evade an unpleasant ending with any variation on that hoary standard "It was all a dream." Nor can mysterious forces appear from nowhere to resolve all the problems, at least not without a great deal of preparation beforehand. (Remember, the deus ex machina was invented in a culture that believed that their gods took an active part in human society: the gods' intervention, though uncommon, was not believed to be unlikely.) On a subtler level, you've agreed to tell a story that has significance—otherwise, why should you or your reader bother?

In terms of setting, you've agreed to provide a plausible, internally consistent world in which your story can take place, one that is appropriate to the story you're telling. The setting shouldn't hinder you in telling your story. It would be difficult to set a novel about whaling in, say, Iowa, and if you're going to subject yourself to that much trouble, you should expect to reap a substantial reward for it. As with plot, you've agreed to use setting fairly: no shifting locations without reason (not just because you went to Venice on your last vacation and you want to use the research), and no vague Everytowns unless that's the point you want to make. You've agreed to take your readers to a specific place—it may be somewhere many of them will have been, like New York City or Disneyland, or it may be somewhere wholly imaginary, but you've agreed to provide enough information to make your world completely real for the course of the story.

In terms of character, the contract is perhaps a little bit more complex. Your contract with your readers does not necessarily oblige you to create likable protagonists or traditional heroes, but it does require you to provide your readers with some reason to stay with these characters' stories. By writing fiction, you have agreed to create characters that your readers can care about. This caring can be as basic as wanting to know what happens next—how a hero like James Bond will escape from the Russians while bedding the girl of the hour. It can be as complex as wanting to understand why a protagonist would lie to himself, or as simple as wanting to be sure that a certain character is destroyed in the end. You still have to play fair—if the character changes in fundamental ways over the course of the story, you have to show those changes taking place; you can't simply pull a new talent or previously unmentioned characteristic out of thin air. The events of the plot should seem to stem directly from the characters' behavior and personality—from their character, in fact. Larry Beinhart argues in *How to Write a Mystery* that much of what is seen as bad characterization is in fact writers forcing characters to act in accordance with a preplanned plot, rather than remaining true to the characteristics already established for them by the author. In a stand-alone novel (as opposed to a novel that is part of a series), the events of the novel should probably be the most important events of the characters' lives.

However, if you want to write science fiction, you have to add several more clauses to this imaginary contract. You have to not only tell a story, place it in a believable setting, and people it with characters that your readers can care about, but also to fulfill a second expectation. You are expected to take your readers into a new world, but one that is still explicitly related to the world in which they live. This brings us to the idea of *extrapolation*. This is what makes SF different from all the other genres, and it's where an SF novel generally stands or falls. Science fiction readers expect an SF novel to connect with what they know of science—and many readers know a great deal. This does not mean that you're restricted only to known and generally accepted facts about the universe; it does mean, however, that you are expected to make a plausible connection to those facts.

Probably the most useful way to look at this idea is to view this "connection with reality" as a continuum rather than a point. On one end is what I think of as the *science fact* novel. These are novels based on a single idea that is accepted as fact by contemporary science, usually one that is a "hot-button" issue in some way—a novel about an outbreak of a new form of Ebola or AIDS, for example, or about possible consequences of researchers' attempts to sequence portions of the human genome. No one would deny that Ebola exists, or that the human genome can be sequenced; the fiction comes from exploring the consequences of those facts. A lot of stories that would fall into this category are actually published outside of the genre (many medical thrillers of the Robin Cook school fit this description), but the basic science fictional connection between fact and story remains.

In the middle of the continuum is the vast majority of what I think of as *science fiction*: novels based on pushing an accepted fact a little further than most scientists would be willing to go. This pushing has to extend in a logical direction (and you should be able to find one or two scientifically literate friends who would agree that it's at least vaguely plausible), but, in general, as long as you can justify your choices, you can take an idea and run with it. At the far end is *science fantasy*, based deliberately on ideas most scientists agree are wrong.

Novels like Arthur C. Clarke's *Rendezvous with Rama* or Hal Clement's *Mission of Gravity* fall closer to the fact end of the spectrum. Both take accepted facts—asteroids have hit the Earth in the past, and probably will again (*Rama*); a planet with a very high gravity in comparison to Earth's would produce certain physical effects (*Mission of Gravity*)—and extrapolate from them to produce a story. Clarke creates a space-based patrol force whose job it is to track and destroy any asteroid on a collision course with Earth (something recently proposed in all seriousness by a group of astronomers). He sends his characters out to deal with the biggest asteroid that has approached the Earth in years (and to find something completely unexpected, but if you haven't read the novel—and it is a truly readable classic—I don't want to spoil the plot). Clement takes the physical imperatives of his high-gravity world, couples them with biology and what we know about evolution, and creates an intelligent species that has evolved on this world and that can—maybe—be persuaded to help visiting earthlings retrieve their stranded survey rocket.

William Gibson's *Neuromancer* and Ursula K. Le Guin's *The Left Hand of Darkness* lie closer to the fantasy end of the spectrum, though both are still unmistakably science fiction. Gibson's human/computer interface, though believable in the context of the novel, nevertheless requires a major leap of technology that is only vaguely described and deliberately left unexplained. The biology of Le Guin's Gethenians, though worked out in meticulous detail, nonetheless requires some hand-waving to explain why they are essentially human. In both cases, while the science is based on generally recognized facts, a major—and unexplained—jump is required to get to the novel itself. Further still along that spectrum are Anne McCaffrey's Pern novels, which—although they have a recognizable science fiction premise—contain elements (the dragons, neomedieval society, and generally low technological level) that are more commonly associated with fantasy.

Finally, at the far end of the spectrum from science fact is *science fantasy*. These books spring from ideas that are acknowledged to be unscientific, unprovable, unlikely, or just plain wrong, but that provide the writers with an interesting starting point. In essence, the writer takes one of these ideas, treats it as though it were true, and frequently derives a fascinating novel from the exercise. A novel that treats cold fusion as a working process would be one example of science fantasy, while Walter Jon Williams's *Metropolitan*—which posits a world in which science itself is different, based on geomancy and the control of an energy called plasm, created from the structure of the novel's massive cities—is another. My own Silence Leigh trilogy (*Five-Twelfths of Heaven*, *Silence in Solitude*, and *The Empress of Earth*), based on the presumption that an archaic scientific model actually works, is a third example, and there are hundreds more.

A couple of caveats are in order, however. There are a few ideas that have become conventions in the field, ideas that really can't be justified in terms of current scientific knowledge, but that nonetheless have become indispensable parts of written SF. Strictly speaking, their use should classify a novel as science fantasy, but only the most die-hard purists actually go that far. The most obvious of these is faster-than-light travel (FTL). According to our current understanding of the universe, it is absolutely impossible for anything to travel faster than the speed of light. Therefore, any travel, human or otherwise, between solar systems will have to be done at something less than that 186,000-miles-per-second speed limit—and that would mean years, often many years, before a ship could travel from one world to another. The sentient or near-sentient robot is another such idea; and the cyberpunk idea of a direct interface between human beings and the world of the computer, pioneered by Gibson, is well on its way to gaining similar status. There are other conventions as well. In part, they exist for the writer's convenience—it's hard to imagine a classic star-spanning galactic empire novel like Dune proceeding at the glacial speeds required by physics. (On the other hand, Robert Silverberg, F. M. Busby, and Ursula K. Le Guin, among others, have written novels that assume only slower-than-light speeds; Le Guin in particular for many years restricted herself to a NAFAL—nearly as fast as light—drive, and structured her fictional societies to take this into account.) However, convenience alone does not explain why these nonscientific ideas became accepted while others did not. (For example, telepathy is also a convenience, but is generally considered to move a book well toward the science fantasy end of the spectrum.) Rather, I think that these conventions have become acceptable not so much because of their scientific plausibility, but because they allow writers to explore issues that are generally considered to be really important. FTL lets writers consider the ramifications of a large and pluralistic society in contact (and often in conflict) with itself, or with others. The sentient or near-sentient robot allows one to question what is and isn't "human." The direct interface with the Net lets an author contemplate the implications of the computer technology that fills the headlines. And so on.

At this point, you may be thinking that science fiction is hardly a genre at all—that these novels I've mentioned have more differences than similarities, and in terms of starting point you're probably right. The similiarity, the genre-ness, if you will, lies in the way those ideas are handled. In each case, the writers treated their ideas as starting points—the classic "what if" that has always been at the core of the genre—and worked out the consequences of their answers to that question. The writers created internally consistent worlds that follow logically from their starting premises. They fulfilled that imaginary contract with their readers: to take them to a place they have never been, a place that is still clearly related to the world in which the readers live.

In this sense, science fiction is very much a fiction of idea or of theme. Without that core idea, without that extrapolation—without the "what if"—a novel can be set in the future, or deal with a classic SF idea like time travel, and still not be what a fan would recognize as science fiction. Conversely, with such an idea, a novel that otherwise conforms to nongenre forms and expectations—like Margaret Atwood's *The Handmaid's Tale*—is, by virtue of its explicit "what "if," unmistakably science fiction. (Her premise is "what if a fundamentalist government was able, in the name of preserving the human species, to decree that women are mere vessels of procreation?")

Does this mean that every SF novel has to have a "what if"? All generalizations are dangerous and some "what ifs" are more complicated than others, but I'm hard pressed to think of an SF novel that doesn't have some form of that question at its core. Is the "what if" the best starting point for a novel—should you have that question firmly in mind before you start writing? The answer to that seems to me to be a qualified "yes—maybe." Writers approach writing in an infinite number of ways. Some people begin with a character who intrigues them, some with a situation, some with an idea or even with an image that evokes something they want to capture and explore. Each of these starting points requires a different set of steps to reach the point at which a neat idea can potentially become a finished novel. (Personally, I start with an image and an idea: I'm constantly doing research—more on that later—and so I'm constantly seeing possible "what ifs," but I can't really use any of them until one sparks an image for me.) As the story begins to gel, though, you should probably ask yourself if the story you want to tell is best served by the science fiction form. If your answer is yes, your "what if" is probably already implicit in your idea; the next step is to tease it out and make it explicit, to articulate it to yourself. This will be useful not only as a marketing tool when you eventually approach agents and/or editors with your manuscript, but also as a way to help sharpen the entire project. You can strip away the interesting but irrelevant ideas (always saving them for later), eliminate characters that don't belong or that detract from the focus (save them, too), and tighten setting and plot to serve the idea better—all before you get too far into a complex manuscript.

Suppose you know that you want to write a book set in the future, but don't have a specific "what if" in mind. One place to start would be to ask what makes this future different from the present. Is there one technological change, or many, or are the changes primarily societal? Somewhere in your answers is the germ of your "what if." Suppose you want to explore what it would be like to be a telepath. That's a pretty good "what if" right there, but you could tighten it further by asking yourself what the limits of your character's telepathy are—for example, does the character read everybody's thoughts all the time, or is she able only to sense emotional states or images without being able to identify the sender? You could also ask yourself if there are other telepaths in this character's world, and how they're treated by nontelepaths. Are telepaths a majority or a minority in this world? Again, your answers to those questions should give you an idea of what your "what if" could be. Suppose you want to take a historical situation and transpose it to the future—according to *The Making of Star Trek*, Gene Rodenberry did precisely that when he created Star Trek's Captain Kirk, taking a British Navy Captain during the Napoleonic Wars (or, more precisely, C. S. Forrester's fictional version of him, Horatio Hornblower) and transferring him to the future. He figured out what it was that he found so appealing about Forrester's character—it was the idea of the ship's captain out on the edges of the world, forced to use his wits and the limited resources of his ship to solve vitally important problems—and found ways to translate that into a future technology. If (for example) you were fascinated by imperial Rome, and wanted to base a future society on that model, a good place to start would be to ask yourself just what it is that interests you. Is it the imperial family (a wild bunch if ever there was one)? Is it a society based on a slavery that isn't predicated on race, and that doesn't leave a permanent underclass? Is it a society where women have no legal standing outside their fathers' or husbands' families, but still manage to run businesses and influence high politics? Each of those questions suggests a different set of changes to get from today to the world of your imaginary future. *Why* would a society revert from contemporary political structures to an empire? Where would slavery come from in a future that includes multiple star systems? Why would a society deprive itself of half its people? As you answer those questions, not only do you come closer to your "what if," but you flesh out the world of your story.

These kinds of questions are integral to the part of SF writing known as world-building, which is just what it sounds like it is, and which I'll be discussing in greater detail in later chapters. Right now, though, we're at the beginning of the process, which is finding an idea that excites you. You want to start with something that turns you on, that makes you want to spend weekends in the library doing the research, and hours at the computer telling your story. Writing is, after all, hard work. There's no point in chaining yourself to a project that is only mildly interesting to you—unless, of course, someone has offered you too much money for you to refuse, and even then, you're going to have some miserable months of it. (Trust me. I've been there.) But for a first novel, or a third or fourth, or for any project that isn't yet sold (and most that are), it's better to start with something that really grabs you. This offers you several advantages—the work is more fun to begin with, and on the really awful days when even your typing works against you, you can still look back at the idea and comfort yourself with the knowledge that there was something there that stirred your soul—and it also helps your writing in some subtle ways. Anyone who's ever taken a writing class will have at some point encountered a teacher or guidebook advising, "write what you know." In SF, it's impossible to do this, at least in the sense in which these teachers usually mean it. ("You used to work at a video dating service? Great material for a novel!") After all, very few of us in the field have ever been into space, and none of us has seen the twenty-first century—we'll get there with everybody else on January 1, 2001, or 2000 if you count new-style. Instead, in SF you're better off writing about something you care about passionately. True, passion can't substitute for knowledge, and you'll still have to do the research you need to get the science and the extrapolation right, but your readers will know when you're connected to your story, and will take fire from your excitement as well. More than that, I believe that really good, genuinely memorable writing happens when you turn that personal passion outward, translating it into a story that touches the same emotions in your readers, drawing them deep into your world. You owe yourself that option, and that chance.

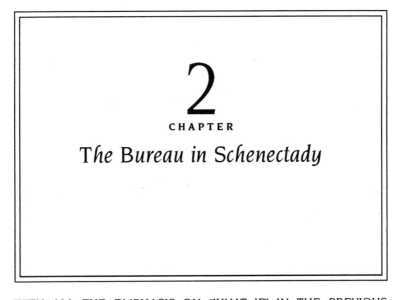

2

CHAPTER

The Bureau in Schenectady

WITH ALL THE EMPHASIS ON "WHAT IF" IN THE PREVIOUS chapter, you probably won't be surprised to hear that the question most frequently asked of science fiction writers is "Where do you get all those crazy ideas?" In fact, the question is so common, and so hard to answer, that a lot of us take refuge in some form of flip answer. (The best of these, which I heard attributed to Isaac Asimov, was the straight-faced explanation that there was an idea bureau, based in Schenectady, that for a modest fee would send aspiring authors a monthly package of a dozen or so ideas, from which they could pick the one they liked best. Last year I drove through Schenectady, and was seized by the desire to find the bureau's off-price outlet store, where it consigned outdated, imperfect, and slightly blemished ideas. In and of itself, this is a pretty good example of the idea process.) Even when writers try to give a serious answer, the process can sound rather odd. Ursula K. Le Guin, in the introduction to her short story "The Ones Who Walk Away from Omelas" (in *The Wind's Twelve Quarters*), comments on the idea's origins:

> The central idea of this psychomyth, the scapegoat, turns up in Dostoyevsky's *Brothers Karamazov*, and several people have asked me, rather suspiciously, why I gave the credit to William James. The fact is, I haven't been able to reread Dostoyevsky, much as I loved him, since I was twenty-five, and I'd simply forgotten he used the idea. But when I met it in James's "The Moral Philosopher and the Moral Life," it was with a shock of recognition. . . .

Of course I didn't read James and sit down and say, Now I'll write a story. . . . It seldom works that simply. I sat down and started a story, just because I felt like it, with nothing but the word "Omelas" in mind. It came from a road sign: Salem (Oregon) backwards. . . . O melas. Omelas. *Homme hélas*. "Where *do* you get your ideas from, Ms. Le Guin?" From forgetting Dostoyevsky and reading road signs backwards, naturally. Where else?

A friend of mine wrote a story because a mutual acquaintance, talking about her plans, said, "But everything may change because it's Jimmy's [her husband's] weekend on the wrecker." The phrase "weekend on the wrecker" struck a chord with my friend; he went home, mulled it over, and produced a story about interstellar search and rescue. My novel *Burning Bright* acquired its final form when I took a rule book for a role-playing game with me and went with my partner to the Iowa Playwrights Festival. In talking to the actors, directors, and playwrights, I was struck by the strong similarities and equally strong differences between what they did and what gamers do, and began to play with that disparity. My book *Trouble and Her Friends* expands the Electronic Freedom Foundation's use of "the virtual frontier" as a metaphor for the Internet and Web into a novel that draws heavily on both the mythic Western and the modern and postmodern criticism of that genre.

So far, all these answers sound more like serendipity than like a method you can rely on, and on one level this is quite true. It's hard to plan for the felicitous word or the brand-new song that gives you exactly the emotional image you want to write about, or the zap when your subconscious connects two unrelated ideas and demands to know what would happen if. . . . On another level, however, those brilliant ideas happen to writers who have prepared for them—who threw themselves in the way of new and interesting things. I think of this as *cultivating serendipity*: making sure that you're in as many places as possible where ideas can strike, and making sure that you're paying attention when you're there. When you're prepared for ideas, both by being actively engaged with the world around you and by finding ways to experience new things, you're more likely to find yourself with a constant source of new ideas.

So, how do you go about cultivating serendipity? For a start, you need to read. Since science fiction is as intimately linked to the contemporary world as any other form of fiction, you should probably subscribe to a good newspaper. A good local newspaper is even better, because you'll have a better chance of assessing the accuracy of its stories on the one hand and of catching some odd human-interest snippet on the other. (I subscribe to two daily papers, a big city daily and my local paper.) Once you've subscribed, read. Start a clipping file to store articles that intrigue you, and flip through it on a regular basis. (I check mine when other projects are going badly.) If you can afford it, subscribe to a good science journal—*Scientific American* is the classic, but may be more technical than you want; *Discover* is a well-done popular science monthly, to name two possibilities—or at least spend one day a month reading them at your local public library. Again, save the articles that intrigue you, and look back over them often: sometimes it takes the collision of two or more articles to give you an idea you can work with. Read other people's science fiction—I hope that sounds obvious—not just to see how they handle craft and style (though you should be doing that, too) but also to see what issues and ideas are nagging at them. Some writers are kind enough to list their source material in an afterword or in their acknowledgments; if they don't, well, at least you will have something to say to them if you meet them at a convention. ("I really enjoyed your book, and I'd like to know more" is usually an excellent way to start a conversation.) Read other kinds of fiction and, of course, read nonfiction. When you find something that interests you, pursue it. Make the time to follow up on it, whether that means doing more research—like tracking down a source article—or just sitting down and thinking through the implications of the idea.

Of course, you can, and should, be doing a lot more than just reading. Keep an eye on the science programs on television and plan to tune in when there's something that interests you. Check them out when you're channel-surfing, too, just in case a topic turns out to be more interesting than you expected. If you own a VCR, try to keep a blank tape handy, just in case you stumble on something completely fascinating; you may be very glad to have a permanent record of that program later. Be sure to get out of the house, too. Go to museums and galleries; go to theater and movies and concerts when you can; take a class or two in something you've never tried before: all these things are great ways of cultivating serendipity, of throwing yourself in front of a moving idea.

Once you have an idea, though, how do you know if it's good enough, and what do you do with it to make it work as a "what if"? The first question is one of those deceptively simple ones that slide away into mush as soon as you try to articulate an answer. A lot depends on where along the fact/fiction/fantasy continuum you want to place your story, and a lot depends on the feeling and tone you want to impart. In general, though, the kind of idea that makes a good "what if" has a recognizable connection to contemporary science and/or society. It also should be big enough to serve as the starting point for a major departure, through gross or subtle changes, from the contemporary world. It should be something that matters to you, too, that excites, intrigues, or annoys you. As discussed in Chapter 1, writing is hard enough work without handicapping yourself with an idea that doesn't captivate you.

Assuming your idea passes those rather nebulous tests, the next step is to turn it into a "what if." As mentioned earlier, one good way to start is to ask yourself what makes your imaginary future different from the present—specifically, what about your idea precipitates those changes? That's pretty easy to answer if your source is something like an article on electronic money or a study of galley warfare. In the first case, you're trying to define the effects of a single technological change on society. How would privately issued electronic cash—as it's usually presented, a kind of "monopoly money" that you buy with real money, guaranteed only by the issuing company—affect the economy and society? Will "e-cash" be more or less stable than "real money"? Will it be safe, but accessible only to the already rich? Will you have to invest in expensive hardware to get it? Is it valid only in the electronic world, or can you spend e-cash at the local mall? When I last visited Old Sturbridge Village in Massachusetts, the bank there was displaying a booklet from the 1830s listing banks that had failed, or whose currency was no longer worth its face value and could be redeemed only at a discount. (It looked a lot like the lists of lost or stolen credit cards that you see at retail stores, actually, right down to the thin, tissue-like paper.) If I were going to pursue the idea of electronic cash, I would probably do some research into that pre–Federal Reserve era, with special reference to the ways in which people could manipulate the money market in the absence of a national bank to regulate the issuing of currency. (I'd also bear in mind a line from the excellent mid-1980s television series Max Headroom: "Credit fraud? That's . . . worse than murder.")

Now, what if your source was the article on galley warfare? Here you're taking a situation that interests you and translating it into the future—isolating its defining characteristics, and figuring out a plausible way to repeat those characteristics in the future. Galley warfare offers some interesting possibilities: galleys were fragile ships—it's no accident that they were used primarily in the relative calm of the Mediterranean Sea. They weren't purely dependent on the wind for power, although the cost (in terms of human effort at the oars) was very nearly prohibitive. Therefore, that human muscle power was usually provided by "expendable" people, slaves or prisoners sentenced to the galleys as their punishment. Galleys also tended to be short-range craft, ships that spent a few days or weeks at sea, and then returned to harbor to rest and refit; in some periods, they put into shore every night rather than brave the open sea. In most periods, they were purely military craft. Merchant ships, by contrast, were broad-beamed, short-hulled ships that relied on sails for power and used the smallest possible crew to make room for cargo.

Of those characteristics, I find the use of galleys as prison ships most interesting, particularly since, in the sixteenth century, the Spanish empire used the galleys to punish people we would consider political prisoners as well as traditional criminals. I'm also intrigued by the idea of warships that have to put into port at frequent intervals. So, why would it work to staff military craft with convicts? And why would those ships have to dock regularly? One possibility would be to postulate an FTL drive that causes serious side effects, effects that you wouldn't want good citizens to have to endure, but that are considered fitting punishment for convicted felons. Those same side effects would force the ships to return to port on a regular basis, to replace injured crew and to allow nonfelon officers (if there are any—and there would almost have to be, in order to keep the ship under government control) to recuperate. Then, how would the military choose the nonfelon officers, given the side effects, and where would their loyalties ultimately lie? Another possibility, moving now to the science fantasy end of the spectrum, would be an FTL drive that is based on some sort of psionics (telepathy or other mental powers), for which the convict crew provides raw power under the direction of one or more nonconvict officers. Still another would be to assume that you need large numbers of people not for the drive system, but for the weapons. These ships are basically missile platforms, and the convict labor is used to control individual missiles in combat, a mission that is somehow dangerous enough that, again, this society doesn't want to waste decent citizens on it. Each of these options offers an explanation for the two characteristics—a convict crew and frequent returns to port—to occur in a starfaring future.

If your inspiring idea is nontechnological, however, it can be a little more difficult to isolate a "what if" by asking what changes it makes in your imaginary future. This is not to say that these ideas aren't a good source of inspiration—sometimes they're the best, because they are linked to people in conflict rather than to static things—but they do require slightly different handling. For example, I clipped two articles recently for my files. One deals with a negative technological change—the absence of technology rather than its presence—and the other is simply an odd human-interest story that piqued my imagination. The first is an article about the Burmese government's efforts to prevent its citizens from accessing the Internet—in this case, by outlawing the "obtaining or sending" of certain kinds of information, possession of a computer with networking capabilities without authorization, and unauthorized computer clubs, among other things. On the one hand, this offers real opportunities for a novel at the science fact end of the spectrum— imagine a high-tech thriller in which much of the thrill is getting the hardware in the first place, even before the characters can access the Net. On the other, I find myself asking what other technologies (or nontechnological solutions) could replace computers and computer networks as a medium for dissent. Both of those would be fascinating and very workable "what ifs."

The second article, an Associated Press report reprinted in my local paper, tells the story of a cabaret musician, a violinist, who—apparently at his mother's urging—masterminded the theft of another violinist's Stradivarius and then used the instrument himself for the rest of his life. The article detailed both the mechanics of the theft and the reason for choosing this particular instrument: its owner also owned a Guarnerius, so he wouldn't be totally deprived of a fine violin. Some of the aftermath included the information that the violinist's widow and daughter were suing each other for the finder's fee paid when the violin was eventually returned to its insurer. There's no intrinsic reason to treat this as a science fiction story (and equally no intrinsic reason not to); however, there may be extrinsic reasons that you want to do so—the simplest and best of which being that you prefer to work in that form. Perhaps, too, you want to use only part of a story, or to use it in a way that you know distorts or misrepresents what really happened. If that's the case, distancing yourself and your story from the reality by moving the story into the future may be a good alternative. In this case, what intrigues me about the newspaper story is the care the musician took to be sure that, although he was stealing the other man's violin, he would not be taking away his only instrument. To me, the dichotomy between the willingness to steal and the desire to do as little harm as possible is an interesting conflict, and that's what I'd like to move into a science fictional setting. This means that the thing stolen should be something that means as much to my protagonist as a Stradivarius can mean to a violinist, or even more. Like the Strad, it should be something intimately entwined with the protagonist's art and profession, and, like the Strad, it should be too rare and/or expensive for the protagonist to acquire one legitimately. Because I often work in the subgenre of SF known as cyberpunk, my first thought is that the stolen item could be a piece of computer hardware, one that would allow the protagonist to experience cyberspace as no other hardware will. Maybe it's unavailable because it's too expensive, or maybe, like a Stradivarius, it's unavailable because only a limited number were ever made. But cyberpunk isn't the only alternative here. The stolen item could be something as large as a spaceship—a magnificent, one-of-a-kind yacht, perhaps, made by a long-dead master of the craft—or as small as an injector containing a nanotech translator "virus" that would allow the infected party to communicate in any language, including that of art. It could make a genuine difference in the protagonist's life and work, or the effect could be purely psychological. The choice depends on the story you want to tell.

This kind of extrapolation is the clearest example of the other way that "what ifs" function in science fiction. Frequently the "what if" is also the central statement of an SF novel's theme, an abstract idea given literal form. In the case of the Stradivarius, the stolen object becomes a way of talking about need—it makes concrete the more abstract question of ends justifying means. The stones in Mary Rosenblum's *The Stone Garden* function in the same way. They are an imaginary art form, a kind of meteorite that can absorb and play back the emotional memories captured from a model and then sculpted by an artist. The stones are at once a symbol of the novel's focus on artistic choice and responsibility and a literal embodiment of that concern.

Another question that arises in talking about ideas and "what ifs" is the question of originality. This isn't a question you necessarily want to get into in the early stages of a project; it's more likely to arise when you show your work to someone else, either in a writing group or a class, or even when you send it out for sale. A common criticism is "I've read this before"—and yet, at the same time, you will also occasionally hear someone say "this is *too* weird; I don't know what to do with it." So where does that leave a writer, besides confused and annoyed? Personally, I think pure originality—originality in the sense that no one has ever thought of this idea before in the history of the world—is somewhat overrated. Mere novelty doesn't guarantee that a "what if" will be fruitful, or even interesting; a really good "what if" can form the core of a dozen totally different novels. The question "what if you had merchant ships in space" produced stories as various as Poul Anderson's *The Man Who Counts* and Andre Norton's *Solar Queen* novels, which are completely different in concept, tone, and handling of character. The existence of the Internet, and speculation on its possible future incarnations—the same basic "what if"—have spawned an entire subgenre. Usually the complaint that a reader has "seen this before" isn't directed *just* at the idea, but at the extrapolation or the plot or the characters, or most commonly all of the above. If you should get this comment, you should take a look at your story to make sure you haven't inadvertently duplicated someone else's ideas and their treatment of them. If that's not the problem, and often a second glance will reveal that, yes, it is, then you need to probe a little deeper. If you can, ask your critic to explain, and if you can stand to hear it, do so—and listen. If you can't interrogate your critic (if, for example, you got a rejection letter from a busy editor, you almost certainly won't be able to get that person's input, and you shouldn't try without an explicit invitation), then you need to take a long, hard look at your story. Have you combined a familiar "what if" with a conventional plot and setting, or a cast of characters that owes more to other people's books, movies, or television shows than to reality? Then, yes, your readers probably have seen all the components of this story before, and you need to rethink one or more parts of your idea before you start your next rewrite. A good rule of thumb is this one: the more familiar a story's "what if," the more original your working out of its consequences must be.

Similarly, the complaint "too weird!" is usually about the entire story, not just about the idea. (It's also one of the complaints you hear from people who just plain don't like science fiction: it's too weird, and they just can't get into it.) In this case, one of the things you should check first is that your idea is logically worked out—that the extrapolation is clear, and you haven't left out something that would clarify your story. If that's not the case, then the issue is probably one of accessibility: the story seems "weird" because you haven't given your readers a way in. Too many changes can be as distracting as too few. A reader bombarded with a totally unfamiliar "what if," changes in dialect, alien names and terminologies, and a dozen other oddities in the first chapter is likely to give up on the story. This is not to say that you can't ask your readers to work with you, or to make an effort to follow a complex or difficult idea; you can, and they will. But you do need to offer points of entry into the story, things that are recognizable and on which readers can rely on as they work out the rest of the story.

Generally, though not universally, when a "what if" is really bizarre, the characters are what pull the reader through. Those characters don't have to be types or, certainly, stereotypes, but they do need to be people that readers can identify with, whose motives they can understand. *Star Wars*, for example, was a movie made for an audience that at the time was hugely unfamiliar with science fiction. The incredible setting—Tatooine, the Death Star, the aliens peopling every scene—was balanced by a relatively simple plot and characters: the young hero, supported by his aging, mystic teacher and his wisecracking cynical friend, has to save the princess and the galaxy. Le Guin's *The Left Hand of Darkness* uses the same technique in a more sophisticated manner. She balances her very alien "what if" (what if there were people who had gender and sexuality only once a month?) with characters that the reader likes, respects, and understands. Both the human Genly Ai and the Gethenian Therem Harth rem ir Estraven are well-intentioned people caught in difficult situations; both want the same thing, and both act consistently out of the best motives. Even though neither one fully understands the other's positions, each one is straining to understand—and the reader identifies with that struggle, and learns a great deal about both societies through it. This is the other side of the rule I cited above: in this case, the stranger the "what if," the more you must provide familiar elements to help your readers to understand the situation.

Finding a "what if" can be one of the most exciting and enjoyable parts of writing science fiction—certainly it's the stage at which you the writer are most free to play with a wide range of ideas, whether they're technological, cultural, or emotionally evocative. It can also be one of the most difficult if you're unwilling to let your imagination roam widely, and there are few things as frustrating as working on a "what if" only to see it fall apart as you explore it. Most of all, though, the "what if"—the idea at the core of the story—is the defining characteristic of science fiction. You can't work in the field without becoming comfortable with extrapolative play.

MIND GAMES

In later sections, I'll be offering some more conventional writing exercises, but it's hard to offer "exercises" that teach you how to make up ideas. Instead, I'm giving a list of suggestions for getting started, a handful of ways of getting your mind into gear. (Or out of a rut: some of these are techniques I use when I'm feeling stale or bored as well as when I'm trying to come up with a new idea.) Some of them will work for you, some of them won't—a couple of them don't work for me, but talented and intelligent writers swear by them. The point is to start thinking like a science fiction writer: to start seeing the possibilities in the mundane.

1. Start a clipping file. You can organize this any way you like. I keep two manila folders in my filing cabinet, one for magazine articles, the other for newspaper clippings (because of size and shape, they're awkward to file together). Other people keep loose-leaf binders; one particularly anal writer of my acquaintance files articles alphabetically by topic in one of those accordion files that are sold to organize correspondence. Try to add to your collection on a regular basis.

2. If you have World Wide Web access, spend an hour or two surfing—without using your "back" button. Start from a search engine for best results (Yahoo has a random site button), and follow the links that interest you, but don't retrace your steps. (OK, you can use the back button if you hit a 404 URL Not Present, or if you get a *really* slow connection.) Feel free to bookmark sites that you want to explore in more detail later, but right now the point is to explore. If you're worried about offensive or sexually explicit sites, don't go there—most sites' subject matter is pretty obvious from the names, and most of the sex sites have a bail-out button you should feel free to use before you get to anything that might offend.

3. The next time you're in a library with open stacks, check out the books in the cases to either side of the books you're looking for. The vagaries of both the Library of Congress and the Dewey Decimal System being what they are, apparently unrelated items are frequently shelved side by side, and you may find something that interests you. If you do, read it. (I found a book of Kabuki scripts this way, got interested in the Kabuki theater, Edo Japan, *ukiyo-e* prints and the "floating world," and ended up using a number of those ideas in a novel called *The Kindly Ones*.) You can do the same thing in your local bookstore, though it

may be more expensive: instead of heading to the section where you usually find your favorite reading material, go to the section to its left instead. (Or the right. Or two over.)

4. If you usually read nonfiction for pleasure, get a novel. If you usually read fiction, find some nonfiction that interests you. If you never read, pick up a book; if you never watch TV, choose a show and give it a try. Do something a little different: the worst that can happen is that you'll be bored for an hour or two.

5. Know and use the resources in your community. If there are museums, visit them, particularly if there are changing exhibits. If there's a university or college, keep an eye out for (often free) lectures that sound interesting, and for other special events that are open to the public. (Our local university recently hosted a Llama and Alpaca Festival.) Bookstores often sponsor reading series and book discussion groups, as well as other one-time events.

6. If you have Internet access, subscribe to newsgroups that interest you—you don't have to post, but you may find interesting information there. You can do the same thing on the commercial services' discussion groups. (This one's not for the squeamish, as the level of verbal aggression can be quite high. I confess it doesn't work for me; I subscribe to only three newsgroups, and I don't read them regularly.)

7. _Go hang out someplace—a coffeehouse, diner, beach, arcade, mall (yes, the mall)—for an hour or two and watch people. Make up stories that explain what they're doing. Be physically discreet and mentally outrageous.

8. Take a class in a subject that's always interested you. Let yourself be a complete beginner again.

9. Buy a phrase book in the language of a country you have no intention of visiting.

10. Play.

Interlude

ROB GATES'S AND MICHAEL CORNETT'S TITLE EXERCISE

THESE FRIENDS OF MINE FOUND A PACK OF TRADING CARDS featuring covers from pulp mysteries of the '30s and '40s—books with wonderfully over-the-top titles like *Satan's Houseboat* or *The Bloody Bride*—and decided to write a series of stories based on the various titles. They made a list of all the titles, cut them up into little slips of paper, and drew one out of a hat. Each one would then write a short story based on that title, and when they were both finished, they'd draw another title and start again.

This is a really good exercise to get you started writing, and to start you thinking about the ideas that become "what ifs." There's no real performance pressure—these are for fun and practice, not for publication; the object is to finish the story, not to set the world on fire. You don't have to use pulp titles, though personally I find them evocative precisely because they're so outrageous. Instead you could use the following:

- album or song titles
- familiar quotations
- literal translations from a phrase book in a language you don't speak
- names of quilt blocks
- street names (there was a street where I grew up called Short Foster Street)
- tarot cards

Any group of five or six related items would work, as long as you find them personally evocative.

The great advantage to this exercise is that it gives you a jump start into the story in the form of the phrase, title, or card but still makes you tell a complete story, i.e., come up with the characters, setting, and plot, and make the reader (in this case, yourself) care about what happens to them. These stories probably shouldn't be long, but should be at least complete scenes, with a beginning, a climax, and a conclusion. The object is to get yourself in the habit of thinking like a writer, and of following through on your inspiration.

Who knows what you may come up with in the process?

VARIATIONS

1. Just to get you started, and to demonstrate that unlikely sources can be weirdly fertile, here are some names of quilt blocks from Jinny Beyer's *The Quilter's Album of Blocks and Borders*: Odd Fellows, Devil's Dark House, Fly Foot, Nameless Star, Broken Dishes, Star of Empire, Stone Mason's Puzzle, Blue Meteors, Variable Star, Coxey's Camp, Devil's Claws, Odds and Ends, Eight Hands Around, Storm at Sea, Spider's Den, Ring of Fortune, Blindman's Fancy, The Disk, Clay's Choice, Patience Corner, The Blockade, Economy, Contrary Husband, The Anvil, Checkerboard Skew, Queen Charlotte's Crown, The Best Friend, Harvest Sun, World Without End, Star and Chains, Captive Beauty, and Blazing Sun.

   They sound a little like space opera to me, but let your imagination take you where it wants to go.

2. Instead of titles, try the personals. Copy a selection of ads or just cut up a newspaper into individual ads—try to get a broad selection, not just Men Seeking Women—then draw at random any two ads. Create one character from each ad and put them into a single story. They can have any relationship to each other—friends, lovers, ex-lovers, teammates, colleagues, rivals, bitter enemies—but they must have a single goal. Again, let your imagination roam.

3
CHAPTER

Getting Started

WORLD BUILDING 101

AN IDEA ALONE ISN'T A STORY. ONCE YOU'VE GOT AN IDEA THAT excites you, you have to work with it to create a setting, characters, and ultimately a plot that brings that idea to fictional life. The idea itself obviously dictates some of your choices, but the choices you make at this stage will also affect the way your plot develops, so it's worth taking time and care with them. Some people find it easier to start with characters, and some with *world building*, the science fictional catch-all term for physical and social settings. Personally, I like to start with the setting, but if you're a person who finds it easier to start from a character, feel free to skip ahead to the next chapter, tackle the characterization ideas and exercises, and come back to the world building afterwards.

Whether you're doing it first or last, however, your goal is the same: to create a physical and social background that supports your story the way sets and costumes support a play. Science fiction as a genre functions by telling an essentially unrealistic story in a realistic fashion. A well-developed, detailed background helps create that realism, facilitating the willing suspension of disbelief that readers want to bring to any novel. A poorly developed setting can break that suspension more quickly than almost any other factor. Setting also supports characterization, whether or not you've worked out your characters first. If you have, your goal is to imagine societies that could produce your characters, and a physical world that will support that society. If, like me, you start with setting, you're letting your imagined reality influence your characters at an almost organic level. Personally, I find that starting with setting helps build in complexity—instead of tailoring worlds to fit my people, I end up creating people who belong in their worlds, and spring from their contradictions and inconveniences. But, whichever way you work, at some point you find yourself playing a giant game of Twenty Questions as you try to figure out how your world should work. The questions that follow are some of the ones you should be asking yourself.

Most of the time, your "what if" already suggests some limits to your setting, and that's the place to start. After all, if your idea involves multiplanetary travel and a human-settled galaxy, you would have to work unreasonably hard to set the story in the near future in, say, Vermont. Conversely, if you're interested in the electronic cash idea mentioned in the previous chapter, it's probably to your advantage to keep things close to the present day and possibly to restrict yourself to the solar system, if not the planet. A story about a new, improved form of FTL drive implies multiple planets even if all the action ends up taking place on shipboard—two factors there that your setting has to account for, a multiplanetary culture and the starship. A story about the first development of FTL, on the other hand, still requires the starship setting, but implies that, if other worlds have been settled at all, they were reached with great difficulty and at slower-than-light speeds. This in turn implies that most of your characters know only one planet well. Your goal is to strike a balance between complexity and complications, to make your story interesting without making telling it unreasonably hard for yourself. This suggests a first question:

WHAT DOES YOUR "WHAT IF" TELL YOU ABOUT ITS SETTING?

In general, you'll find that core ideas function both positively and negatively, requiring certain things and ruling out others—I find it helpful to think of it as drawing a line that defines the outer boundaries of the story, rather than as a set of limits.

Another good question to ask early in the world-building process is the following:

WHAT ARE THE PHYSICAL LAWS THAT OPERATE IN YOUR WORLD?*

In other words, you should know roughly how every invented element in your story works—*even if your characters don't.* Each of your invented technologies will have limits and rules, as well as the advantages you need to make your idea work; you need to have a firm grasp of those before you begin plotting. The wildest extrapolation can be made to work (at least for the length of a novel) by meticulous attention to detail and an obsession with consistency; on the other hand, an inconsistent science and/or technology will destroy your readers' faith in the story faster than almost anything else. After all, this is *science* fiction: one of the basic expectations is that you will follow scientific assumptions about method, causality, and connection even if you take the "science" to extremes.

The fact that your characters are ignorant of their worlds' workings is no excuse. If anything, when a story is about the discovery of some new science or technology, you have to work harder to achieve the same level of consistency. First, your readers know that the story is about solving a problem, and will be following your logic more closely because they're engaged with your characters in figuring out what's going on. Second, you have to convey most of the information indirectly. None of the characters knows for certain how this new discovery works (solving that problem is what the book is about, after all), and some characters' guesses are likely to be wrong—but you have to make those guesses plausible and yet not contradict your eventual solution. The more you know about your invented sciences and technologies, the easier it will be to persuade your readers to spend time with your story.

HOW BIG IS YOUR WORLD?

In this case, "world" isn't limited to a single planet; it's the world of the story, the entire setting, including the parts that are never described but are only referred to in the narrative. By definition, worlds are big: you need room for your story. Even the most

---

*I'm indebted to my friends in the CoastLine SF Writers Group for this and the following questions.

claustrophobic settings achieve a greater effect by being contrasted to the greater world outside. Think of the film *Fantastic Voyage* or the novel *The Boat* (or its filmed versions). In each case, the characters' enclosed world is all the more impressive for knowing a little bit about what's waiting for them on the outside. Worlds are big in another sense: they generally contain a variety of different, smaller settings. Even Arrakis, the desert world of Frank Herbert's *Dune*, wasn't just endless sand—the novel explores both the cities and the various kinds of desert wilderness—and in any case a sizable part of the action takes place off-world, on other planets. If you decide that your story requires a world that is nothing but ocean or nothing but desert, remember that deserts and oceans, and all the other natural habitats, contain innumerable variations: after all, the Caribbean and the North Sea are both ocean environments. The more space your setting contains, the more room you have to tell your story. Even a small-scale story needs *scope*.

HOW BIG IS YOUR CHARACTERS' WORLD?

Planets are big, and solar systems are even bigger. Even in the most sophisticated societies, your characters will rarely be familiar with all of the possible places. One way of adding verisimilitude to your settings is to invent a few locations that won't appear in the story. These could be important planets that your characters will never visit, a capital city, waste or wildlands that surround the main settings, or anything else that helps set the tone of your plot. You can then refer to them as the characters would refer to them—as mythic places whose meanings you define, as places your characters desperately want to visit, or as desperately want to avoid, even as names that they've heard and know little about. These brief references add extra dimension to a story, and help create the illusion of a realistic setting.

One caveat is in order, however. These references have to serve the story; if they're inserted just because you like your invention, the narrative will quickly bog down in detail. Instead, you should use these "off-screen" places to reinforce the main thrust of your story. For example, in his three Anthony Villiers novels (*Star Well*, *Masque World*, and *The Thurb Revolution*), Alexei Panshin's characters never once set foot on the planet called Nashua, and Panshin never describes it in any detail, but that planet literally sets the tone for all three novels. They take place on the fringes of the Nashuite Empire, in a society in which everything cultured and important comes from Nashua. By the middle of the first book, "Nashua" has become for the reader a shorthand reference to everything the characters aspire to be—as it is for the characters themselves. You don't need to know anything more about Nashua than that. In my own *Dreamships* and again in its sequel *Dreaming Metal* there are a number of references to the "Urban Worlds." I spent some time defining them to myself—they're a group of eighteen to twenty planets that are close enough to each other to permit cheap and easy travel among the group (generally speaking, interstellar travel is relatively expensive in these novels), and that therefore dominate the overall culture. I know the names of many of them, and something about their major physical features. However, almost none of this gets used in either novel. What does get used is the *idea* of the Urban Worlds—a "First-World" culture in contrast to the "Second-World" setting of the novels—and the names.

Is it worth the effort to invent places that you'll never use? I think so. I've never found a better way to create the illusion that you're culling selective details from a setting that you see fully. After all, it's not entirely an illusion.

WHAT ARE THE DOMINANT PHYSICAL FEATURES OF YOUR WORLD?

In other words, what are the major features that your characters cannot avoid? Is it a desert, as in *Dune*, or an ocean, a forest, the vacuum of outer space, a city, a starscape, storms, hot or cold climate, a double or triple sun, massive gravity, or something else? Obviously, if you pick something big, like a double sun or an eccentric planetary orbit that creates long-term climatic shifts (Dan Simmons and Joan Vinge have both worked with that idea), the consequences to your story are equally large and dramatic. Even if the story isn't about the setting, the setting has an enormous impact on everything that happens in it. However, relatively minor changes from the terrestrial norm also have an effect on the story, and deserve to be worked out in detail. On the one hand, working through the consequences protects you from mistakes (and science fiction readers tend to be knowledgeable and to have extremely long memories), but, more important, it gives you a chance to see possibilities that might not have occurred to you otherwise.

Suppose, for example, that you want to set your story on a planet on which the predominant color is blue. Sky and sea are both blue, the soil and rocks have a blue-grey tone, and the vegetation is all blue as well. (Maybe your main interest is changes in perception in this monochromatic setting, or you want to echo a "blue" feeling in the main narrative.) It's not hard to make air and water appear blue—that's the terrestrial default, after all—and bluish rocks occur on Earth as well. Blue dirt, however, is a little harder, and all-blue plants are harder still. One way to justify the blue ground would be to assume a predominance of minerals that look bluish once they're exposed to atmosphere. You can justify blue plants in a similar way, assuming that whatever functions as chlorophyll in their leaves looks blue, the way the chlorophyll looks green. It shouldn't be too hard to find a suitable mineral, or to invent something that serves your purpose, but that choice raises a new set of possibilities. For one thing, is that compound safe for your human characters? If not, what are its effects, and are they short-term or long-term? If human beings can't eat the native vegetation, what are you going to feed them? If I were interested in creating a real feeling of misery on this blue world, I would probably make the compound fairly toxic, so that my characters were forced always to stay inside their shelters or vehicles—with a beautiful, dreamy-looking, deadly landscape, all shades of blues, always in sight and forever inaccessible. The same choice would heighten the issues of perception: it is hard to see a purely monochromatic world (think of blurred black-and-white photographs), and not being able to investigate it directly just compounds the problem. You could also decide that something in the atmosphere creates the illusion of blue color, and work out the consequences of that choice. Of course, you don't have to decide that the color is harmful, or that it's anything except different—"blue grass" may, for example, be the simplest way to distinguish one of several planets on which your story takes place—but when you take the time to look at the further consequences of a choice, you open yourself up to new insights.

I discovered this when I was working on The Kindly Ones, which I had proposed to Jim Baen at Baen Books. He was interested in the idea, but was concerned that it was too low-tech, and suggested that I set the story on several different planets instead of on just one. I accepted the low-tech criticism, but didn't like the idea of multiple planets, since I needed my characters to be able to travel between the various locations fairly quickly. I offered to use the moons of a gas giant instead, and he accepted the book. At this point, I had to go back to the setting and work out the interactions of three moons, their parent planet, and the local star. My good friend and fellow SF writer Don Sakers offered to help me with the astronomy, and together we came up with a workable solar system, with moons that were close enough to the sun and their parent planet to support life in a climate that I liked. However, as we worked with the system, we found some unexpected results that turned out to be perfect for the story I was telling. For one thing, the parent planet, a gas giant called Agamemnon, was big, and it looked big in the skies of its moons—about eighteen degrees in apparent diameter from the nearer moon, Orestes. (Our full moon, by contrast, appears to cover about a degree of sky.) It has phases, just like our moon, and it's pretty much always visible in the lunar sky. In addition, the proximity of the moons to Agamemnon and each other made for a strong tidal resonance that produced volcanic activity on Orestes every twenty-four days. And, finally, the Oresteian day was 142.32 hours long—about 71 hours of daylight, followed by about the same of night—and Agamemnon eclipsed its star on a regular cycle, bringing a few extra hours of night in the middle of Orestes' long day. I already knew that a primary social issue in the novel was the existence of people who had been declared legally dead for breaking their society's strict codes of behavior. I used that day/night cycle, and the eclipse at its center, to reinforce the division between the living and the legally dead "ghosts," deciding the legally dead could act legally only during the night and the eclipse. The regular volcanic eruptions allowed my protagonists to escape from Orestes at one crucial point in the novel. If I hadn't worked out the consequences of settling three moons that orbited a gas giant—if I had just assumed that things would be the way I wanted them—I wouldn't have known about these possibilities, and the book would have been poorer for it.

In this instance, the unavoidable feature of the setting was the fact that the story took place on a moon; in *Dune*, it was the desert of Arrakis; in James Blish's *Cities in Flight* it was the city of New York, cut off from everything by the encasing fields of the "spindizzy drive" and wandering the universe; in *Neuromancer*, it was the Net itself. Each of these major features—each of these authors' choices—in turn influenced a host of lesser features, adding detail to the stories. Once you have your major features in place, it's time to ask some more questions:

WHAT IS THE CALENDAR LIKE?
WHAT IS THE CLOCK LIKE?

Planets vary a great deal from Earth, and the actual length of both year and day is dependent on each world's orbit. In fact, the chance of a world having a twenty-four-hour day exactly like Earth's is pretty slim, as is the chance of its having a 365-day orbit. You may find it useful to calculate the length of year and day, and to play with the consequences—a slow rotation, resulting in a long day and night, produces a very different society from a fast day/night cycle. A world where orbit and rotation are synchronized, like our moon, creates a permanently daylit side, a permanent night side, and possibly a band of twilight between the two. This might be a difficult place to settle, given the resulting temperature differences, but potentially fun to explore. You could even play with the idea of incompatible calendars—imagine updating Gilbert and Sullivan's *Pirates of Penzance* so that our hero's dilemma stems not from being born on February 29, but being born on a world with a much longer year than the one on which the contract was written. Joan Vinge's *The Outcasts of Heaven Belt* uses the hour as the basic unit of reckoning, producing a society that thinks in terms of "kilohours" rather than days or years. This is perfectly logical in a society that lives in an asteroid belt, where the important factor is not place but the (constantly changing) distance between locations.

You don't have to use a different calendar and clock, of course—conventionally, you can simply allude to dates in "Earth years" or some equivalent (I use "standard years" myself, most of the time) and give characters' ages in "biological years" or the like. The same goes for time: you can establish a "standard" twenty-four-hour day and refer to that alone. In fact, there are times when adding a non-standard clock or calendar is just creating one too many items for readers to remember. (The first draft of my own *Shadow Man*, which describes three unfamiliar genders, each with its own new set of pronouns, as well as two conflicting dialects, also included a twenty-six hour planetary day. I deleted those references from the second draft because the long day was just too much to keep track of on top of the new pronouns and the invented dialects.) This is always a judgment call, and in making that decision, I find it useful to remember a concept proposed by Ellen Kushner during a panel we were both on at Arisia. She argued that every novel has a fixed "strangeness budget," a finite number of new or unfamiliar things that readers can absorb and understand without losing track of the story. Adding too many ideas purely for the sake of novelty risks overspending that budget. If there are too many other things going on, or if the "what if" itself is very strange, you should probably keep the secondary ideas and features as recognizable as possible.

WHAT IS THE CLIMATE LIKE?

This is another feature that is likely to be profoundly affected by your dominant physical features, if it isn't the dominant feature itself. It affects the questions that follow, and is itself affected by questions of planetary orbit, rotation, and distance from the parent sun, as well as the characteristics of the sun and planet themselves. Again, you don't have to make things profoundly different from Earth, but it often adds plausibility to a nonterrestrial setting to create an extra season or to assume a smaller or wider range of seasonal variation. It's also worth your while to remember that even in our own country there are strange seasons that fall outside the simple spring-summer-autumn-winter pattern: California has monsoon rains, while Vermont has mud season. People also perceive the same seasons differently depending on their profession and location: when I was growing up in Arkansas, early March was spring, while here in New England, "spring" doesn't start until the end of April. "Tornado season" has been replaced by "hurricane season." For some of my friends, "spring" begins when they can plant seeds outdoors. Farmers perceive weather and seasons differently from fishermen; urban people see them differently from rural people, and so on. Nonhuman characters are likely to see "seasons" differently from human characters, too. It's worth a few moments of thought to consider how your characters might view the seasons of your world, whether they break them up into more or fewer seasons, or if there's a period of unusual weather—storm or calm or something else—that warrants being set aside in people's minds. Even if you end up using only a few words, putting in a few brief seasonal references can add to the illusion of realism. And if you pick the seasons and/or weather well, they can reinforce the story the way few other images can.

WHAT IS THE DOMINANT VEGETATION? THE DOMINANT ANIMAL(S)?

If the answers are "none," how do you feed your character(s)? If you're setting the story on another planet, has it been *terraformed*—remade to make it as Earth-like as possible—or is it more or less the way it was when the first human settlers landed? Can human beings eat the vegetation or the animal life? (Realistically speaking, the chance of evolution on an alien planet duplicating the chains of molecules that produce food plants edible to human beings is fairly small—but this is one of the times when the genre's conventions raise the odds for you.)

WHAT IS THE FOOD CHAIN, AND WHERE DO YOUR CHARACTERS FALL ON IT?

You don't have to go into too great detail here, though it's important in terms of plausibility to build a food chain that can sustain everything that you need for the story. For example, if you need massive herbivores, you certainly need large numbers of plants for them to eat throughout the year (or some reason that they don't eat during the winter). And you probably also need a population control for them—perhaps a predator, or a slow reproductive cycle. If you want intelligent, aggressive carnivores, you need something for them to hunt—and that something needs to be clever and tough in its own right, to produce intelligence and aggression in its predators. If your characters aren't at the top of the food chain, well, that makes them *prey*, with all the appropriate consequences. You also may want to spend some time thinking about what your characters eat. Food habits can be a useful tool in defining both the characters and their world. However, their tastes need to be supported by their setting— or if their favorite food isn't readily available, you need to know that, and figure out how they get it. (Imported food is generally expensive, and the farther it has to come, the more expensive it is.)

WHAT IS THE "AVERAGE" MODE OF TRANSPORTATION?

Another way of looking at this is to ask yourself how your characters get around, and how long it takes them to get from one location to another. The scale of those answers depends a lot on the size of the story's immediate setting—there's a huge difference between the "average" mode of transportation in a near-future, cyberpunk novel and a novel set in a hundred-planet interstellar federation thousands of years in the future. Mass transit—maybe even familiar subways and buses—may suffice for the first, while the second almost requires quick and efficient faster-than-light travel. Another question is whether transportation would be individual, like cars in contemporary society, or communal, like airplanes or buses, and whether it's expensive or cheap. If you're dealing with an interstellar society, you'll have to decide between slower-than-light and faster-than-light travel, and then work out the basic mechanics of your chosen mode. For some stories, it may be appropriate, even necessary, to go into great detail, working out things like acceleration tables, fuel sources, rates of consumption, the specific physical model that makes a particular FTL drive work, and so on, but in most cases the things that you need to know are how long it takes and how much it costs. Personally, I enjoy working out FTL drives, and even those novels that don't emphasize FTL travel have a page or two of background notes so that I know how the system works. I think this adds to the illusion of reality: I can refer to the FTL drive apparently in passing, and still know that all my references are consistent with an unstated model.

Once you've considered these questions, and any others that occur to you—and there are many other possibilities, depending on the particular thrust of your story—you need to put it all together. In other words, how do all these physical facts affect your characters and their story? At this point, you may run into problems. Ideas that seemed exciting in the abstract may seem to impose insurmountable obstacles, and you may feel as though you've wasted all the work you've done. I'd encourage you not to abandon a setting too soon, however. Sometimes working around an apparent inconvenience can add a new layer to your plot. I confess, I wasn't at all happy at the idea of shifting the story that became *The Kindly Ones* from a single planet to three moons. I really needed my characters to be able to get from one location to another at reasonable speeds, and the trip from one moon to another was simply too long to be undertaken easily. However, as Don and I worked out the details of the system, the visual and imagistic advantages of the three-moon system began to outweigh the inconvenience, and I ended up reworking a part of the plot in order to keep the images that were proving to be very powerful. That's an extreme example, and of course there will be times when nothing will salvage a part of a setting, but it's important not to abandon ideas too quickly.

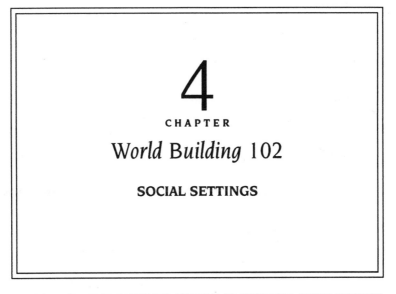

4

CHAPTER

World Building 102

SOCIAL SETTINGS

OF COURSE, THE PHYSICAL WORLD IS NOT THE ONLY SETTING of any novel. People, characters, generally live in societies— Robinson Crusoe, marooned on his island, was still very much a product of his society, and replicated many aspects of it in his relationship with Friday and with the island itself. Tarzan was raised by apes, in a nonhuman, animal society created by Burroughs. Even a spaceship with a crew of one person is a society of a kind, and in any case, it's influenced by the society that built the ship. As with physical settings, your "what if" will generally provide some boundaries for the society of your story, and that's probably the best place to start the game of questions.

WHAT DOES YOUR "WHAT IF" IMPLY ABOUT ITS SOCIETY?

To go back to a "what if" mentioned in Chapter 2, the concept of electronic cash implies a number of things about the society in which its story would take place. For one thing, it is a society that is familiar with and to a certain extent dependent on computers; for another, it has a complex economy, and probably a sophisticated system of credit within that economy. Questions of trust and mistrust and face value vs. real value are extremely important, and probably spill over into more than just matters of money. The galley idea, on the other hand, implies first an interplanetary and probably an interstellar society and, second, a society that has a strong military component. That in turn implies an ongoing need for the military—an enemy, internal or external—or a shift in military function to exploration and policing. The use of convict labor on these ships implies a "criminal element" large enough to staff them, and that in turn suggests a desperate underclass, or perhaps political dissent, or even a class of psycho- or sociopaths that the government is trying to control by drafting them. All of those options suggest in turn a world in which the government is extremely active in attempting to shape society. Note that this says nothing about whether that intervention is benevolent or malevolent in its intentions—that's your choice, as the writer—but, given the nature of the "what if," it would be hard to avoid an active government.

Once you've sorted out the shape that your "what if" gives to its society, you need to fill in the details. I usually start by asking myself questions that focus on the power to affect others' actions. This helps me define the position of both my protagonist(s) and antagonist(s), because they both have to act in the context of the invented society. You can start from almost anywhere, of course, but I find it useful to think in these terms because it puts the focus on active rather than passive characters.

WHO HOLDS POLITICAL POWER IN YOUR SOCIETY?
WHO HOLDS ECONOMIC POWER?
ARE THEY THE SAME?

Who's in charge here? Individuals? A group? Several groups? One or more corporations? No one? I've made the distinction between political and economic power because, although the two often overlap, they don't have to be identical, and the two kinds of power function very differently. To cite an example from our own world, a corporation that wishes to see a law passed by Congress proceeds differently from a member of the government who wants to see the same law passed. Conversely, political power may not bring wealth directly to its holders, and people with political power earn their money differently from people whose power springs directly from their economic control. If you choose one or more individuals, you have to justify their holding power; you also have to consider the nature of their power, and its sources. For example, monarchies gain power from a mystical belief in the hereditary right of some specific family; dictatorships, on the other hand, generally spring from an individual's control of either the power of coercion (the army, for one) or the power of reward (a society in which everyone is employed by an individually owned company places everyone completely at the mercy of that individual). Groups (clans, classes, castes, corporate entities, etc.), like individuals, tend to hold power because they are, or were, perceived to perform a function—and don't forget the possibility of divisions within the group itself!

If the same person or persons hold both economic and political power, the conditions are good for creating an oligarchy, with a closed class holding tight to its control of society. If very different people or groups are involved, then you need to decide if they're going to work together, or if they are in competition for dominance in your society. If they're working together, what makes them willing to cooperate? An outside enemy? A hostile environment? A common belief system? A sense of common good? Are there issues on which cooperation is impossible, or are the groups generally able to find a compromise position? If they're in competition, what's at stake—what will the eventual winner gain by winning? Is there anything that would force them to cooperate? How much does this competition affect the average citizen? A lot of these questions offer possibilities for instant conflict as well as sources of ongoing tension within your narrative.

WHAT IS THE HIERARCHY OF POWER IN YOUR SOCIETY? OF STATUS? DO THEY COINCIDE, AND TO WHAT DEGREE?

Another way of phrasing this question is to ask which groups and people are valued, and which are ignored. Are power and/or status based on fixed (or difficult to change) factors such as family connections, gender, talent, physical appearance, order of birth, DNA factors, computer lottery, and so on? Or are they based on more mutable factors like money, friends, examination results, special skills, and/or education? Can individuals move from one level of the hierarchy to another? Is such movement easy or difficult, complicated or simple? When hierarchies of status and power don't match, you get interesting tensions and potential conflicts. Imagine, for example, a society that values rulers and farmers, and considers merchants to be parasites—but in which an economic change has placed most wealth in the hands of the merchant class, so that the high-status classes are dependent on the low-status group for economic survival. (This is an exaggeration of the situation in seventeenth- and eighteenth-century Japan.) Or imagine its converse, in which the people who actually have power conspire to give status to a different group—maybe one that once had real power, or maybe one that most people feel *should* have power but no longer does except by the deference of the other groups. (Present-day European nobility springs to mind.) Again, this kind of mismatch can add to a story's conflict as well as providing an interesting and realistic complexity.

WHAT IS THE LEGITIMATE OR OFFICIAL SOURCE OF POWER? WHAT IS THE ACTUAL SOURCE OF POWER?

When the answers to these questions are the same, you have a fairly stable society, even when the answer seems immoral or unpleasant. A society that survives by piracy and recognizes the most successful pirates as its most powerful citizens and leaders is at least united in its understanding of how the world should work. A society that espouses restraint and service to society but rewards selfishness and ostentatious display with great wealth, on the other hand, has a real conflict between its vision of society and its reality, and is far less stable.

The next group of questions is a little more specific than these have been, and are intended to help you flesh out the bare bones of the power structure. They are intended to help you get a fix on the various elements of your society. You don't have to explore all of them in great detail (though I find that fun), but you do need to work out answers to the question most affected by your "what if." For example, if you were using the electronic cash idea, you would need to know a lot about the financial system and almost as much about the general economy. If you were using the galleys idea, you would want to know what that society considered to be its inviolable laws and customs. However, I'd encourage you to give all these issues some attention: you never know when something you hadn't expected to be important will suddenly give you new and vital insight into your imaginary world.

SOCIETIES ARE COMPLEX, AS WORLDS ARE BIG: IS THERE MORE THAN ONE SOCIAL GROUP WITHIN YOUR SOCIETY, AND WHAT IS THEIR RELATIONSHIP TO THE OTHERS? WHAT DO ALL GROUPS IN YOUR SOCIETY HAVE IN COMMON, AND WHAT DEFINES THEIR CRUCIAL DIFFERENCES?

This is actually a way of avoiding one of the most common problems in SF, the unbelievably monolithic planetary society. (It's the social parallel to the one-feature planet.) Most societies contain a number of different groups, defined by everything from religion to ethnic background to economic status to gender. Fundamentalist Islamic society, for example, treats women and men as separate groups that should not come into contact except under specific and special circumstances, and as a result men and women effectively live in different societies. Within the United States, race is a clear divider within the larger society; not too long ago, regional identity was another strong divider, and remains so under certain circumstances. It's worth your while to consider where these internal divisions would occur in your imaginary society, both in the interests of realism, and in order to provide a complex background that can produce understandably complex characters. (If you started with the characters, this process will help justify the complexities you've already imagined.)

If you're having trouble thinking of differences (it can be hard enough coming up with a single society, never mind several subgroups within it), try looking at your own life. Your identity as a member of a family is different from your identity as a worker or student, and different again from your identity as an artist or as a citizen. To give you a quick example, I'm a member of my local Residents' Association, *and* a writer, *and* a member of a local band's entourage; the middle-class homeowner overlaps oddly with the novelist and with the webmaster (which is what I do for the band). I am viewed differently by my peers in each of these groups; my status and behavior within them are different, but I'm legitimately a part of each. And that doesn't even begin to address the bigger cultural identities, like being a lesbian—or an expatriate southerner in a small New England town. Your "what if" will suggest some obvious differences (electronic cash suggests haves and have-nots; the galleys suggest criminals and honest citizens); your task then is to explore each of these groups, and their overlapping points, to help build your larger society.

WHAT ARE THE BASIC RULES OF YOUR SOCIETY? WHICH OF THESE RULES CAN BE BROKEN? WHICH ARE INVIOLABLE?

Every society has certain basic rules (laws, customs, and beliefs) that everyone knows and follows. These assumptions may never have been articulated, and they may not be carried through in all cases—or there may be serious disagreements about interpretation—but everyone knows that these conditions *should* be true. (For example, in *The Great Gatsby*, at least part of the conflict comes about because of a fundamental conflict between the cultural belief that all men are created equal and the cultural reality that some men are more equal than others.) In my own *Night Sky Mine*, the fictional society placed an extremely high value on identity, on having a place in society. Even the subgroups that overtly rejected that belief were influenced by it, replacing the stable identity based on employment valued by the "mainstream" group with membership in individual Traveler bands—a different version of the same need for identity and place.

These rules usually reflect the "what if" in some way, too, either directly or as a response to the questions raised by the core idea. In *Night Sky Mine*, for example, the emphasis on identity lies in opposition to the main idea: what if computer programs became so complex that the only way human beings could manipulate them was to think of them as some kind of animal, and to "breed" them for the jobs at hand? The society of the novel was completely dependent on the "invisible world" of its computer networks, but at the same time knew that it could not describe or define these crucial programs except by a language that was acknowledged to be purely a convenient fiction. As a result of this core uncertainty, people demanded more certainties in the visible world. Identity became the crucial part of that certainty.

WHAT IS THE BASIS OF YOUR ECONOMY?

In other words, what are the major industries, and are they served by human, animal, nonhuman, or machine labor? In many ways, the question of who does the work is more important than what the work actually is, at least in terms of world building. To make a gross distinction, work is viewed very differently when it is something that every adult is expected to perform than when all work is performed by robots. Under the latter circumstances, you would have to find some other way for people to define their purpose in life—and you'd have to decide whether "work" (the production of necessary goods and services) has become an esoteric speciality of robot programmers, a dirty secret that nobody talks about (perhaps with groceries arriving in the middle of the night, concealed from the neighbors), or something else entirely. Nonhuman labor could mean aliens, or biologically human beings who are not perceived as fully human. (Think of the pre–Civil War court decisions in this country that allowed slaves to be counted as three-fifths of a man for tax and representation.) "Animal" could be defined in similar ways—Frank Herbert plays with that idea a little in *Dune* when the Bene Gesserit Mother Superior tests Paul before acknowledging him to be human.

A corollary to this question is whether or not your population is sufficient to support your economic model. (I mention this because I've tripped myself up on this more than once.) This doesn't have to be approached with a great deal of precision, but you want to watch out for contradictions like the newly settled, sparsely populated world that needs massive amounts of cheap human labor in order to prosper. That big a mismatch would require drastic solutions, and drastic solutions belong at the center of a novel rather than on the periphery.

This is a parallel to the idea that the events of a novel should be the most important events of the main characters' lives to that moment. The bigger a problem looms in your readers' minds, the more it deserves to be resolved onstage, through the course of the novel, rather than being relegated to a few paragraphs of exposition. By setting up a serious contradiction, one that demands complex solutions to make your society work, you create the expectation that the contradiction will be resolved (or at the very least explored) through the events of the novel. If you don't meet that expectation, your story is likely to feel unbalanced, not fully satisfying. Big problems and complex solutions are what novels are all about.

HOW MANY LANGUAGES ARE THERE?

Is there just one language, or are there several, with one (or none) dominant? Is there an invented language, or a pidgin or Creole, that everyone uses to communicate with people outside their linguistic group? Is there one language for education (and educated people), that transcends national, cultural, and even planetary boundaries? Latin, as the language of the Catholic Church, the source and repository of most education (and educated people), functioned this way in the European Middle Ages. In fact, being able to read Latin, however poorly, was presumed in many criminal codes to make a person a member of the clergy, and therefore immune to secular law—an interesting possibility for a future society. (It could work rather well with the galley idea, actually.) Is one language privileged, its speakers accorded higher status, or is this a contested issue?

WHAT IS THE FINANCIAL SYSTEM?

Is the monetary system reliable? Is there a single currency, or are there many different monies in circulation? Does the government regulate the system, or does a laissez-faire attitude prevail? Is any currency stable? Is this a capitalist, socialist, communist, communalist, merchantilist, libertarian, or fascist economy—or something else again? Is there credit, and how available is it? An interesting possibility would be to follow the seventeenth-century French model and establish an official currency that exists only on paper, as a record-keeping device, and allow the money that actually circulates to be something very different. (This would make an interesting variation on the electronic money idea: one could assume that the electronic money was the "official" money, but that anyone without access to that, or dealing in denominations smaller than, say, the equivalent of a twenty-dollar bill, would have to use some other, makeshift "real" currency.) As always, of course, your choices should reinforce the theme and overall feeling of your story. In cyberpunk novels, where the splintering of institutions is a major theme, you often see a concern with multiple currencies and their fluctuating values: the unreliable money reflects the unreliability of almost every other institution. (If you're a role-playing gamer, you might be interested in the GURPS* supplement *Cyberworld*, which makes unstable currencies a major part of the game. It's a quick-and-dirty, but very workable, introduction to the concept.) In novels of grand politics, however, the financial system is rarely explored in any detail. Both the neofeudalism of *Dune* and the major corporations in Heinlein's *Citizen of the Galaxy* are assumed to function similarly to such entities in our own world precisely because the books are about issues of personal power in which economics would be a distraction.

WHAT IS THIS SOCIETY'S BASIC UNIT?

Is society organized around the individual? A biological family (or clan, or tribe)? A congregation? A household? The crew of a space-ship? An arbitrarily assigned address? A company, or a division within a corporation? The nuclear family of parents and children? A related question is "What is this society's definition of a family?" Is it, for example, an economic unit as well as a biological and/or social one? A further corollary, and a question that is often overlooked, is "Who takes care of the children, and is that position valued or unimportant?" Marge Piercy's *A Woman on the Edge of Time* in fact weaves a fascinating and very alien-seeming story just by placing that question at the center of her novel. The default value for the basic unit of most SF is that of our own society, the individual, but there are innumerable other possibilities. As always, however, the more unfamiliar your basic unit is, the more important it should be to the story.

I've focused a lot on the possibilities of disjunction, of mismatched expectation and reality, because I have found them to be

---

*GURPS stands for "generic universal role-playing system," Steve Jackson Games' primary role-playing game. The name started as a joke, but stuck.

fruitful sources of conflict for my own novels. The structuralist school of history argues that the most important things about any society can be seen at the boundaries, at the divisions between proper and improper, acceptable and unacceptable, legitimate and illegitimate, mad and sane. (A structuralist historian would, for example, analyze shifting definitions of madness in order to determine socially acceptable behaviors, or prosecutions for illicit sexual activity to determine how the definition of appropriate sexual behavior has changed over time.) As a writer, I've found that idea of looking for boundaries and stress points to be extremely useful both in building fictional societies and then in creating plots that seem to grow organically from the physical setting and the society.

Of course, focusing on stress points and contested issues runs the risk of creating what seem to be contradictions within your fictional society. This can be overdone—you want a society that is plausibly complex, not incomprehensible—but in general, I find that a few contradictions don't spoil the world building, but in fact actively add not only to the imaginary setting, but to the story itself. If you stay within the limits of your "what if," the contradictions that you discover as you invent your society may actually be the source of your story's conflict—or at the very least can be used to sharpen the conflict.

For example, when I was working on my novel *Dreamships*, I began with the question, "What if a nominally democratic, pluralistic society that is completely dependent on complex, near-intelligent computer programs were suddenly confronted with a genuinely intelligent program that it must, by its own rules, treat as equal to a human being?" However, as I developed the society further, it became clear that a large section of the human population didn't have the full human rights that logic demanded society extend to any true artificial intelligence. In other words, the society was nominally democratic, believing in complete equality, while at the same time it relied on a contract labor pool—people who did not have the same rights as everyone else—to maintain its economy. I was able to use this apparent contradiction to focus the story even more closely on the real question: what is a person? The issue for the characters became the question of whether or not they personally could accept that the artificial intelligence (AI), Manfred, was true AI, and therefore a person, when there were so many people who were denied that status. The contradiction within the fictional society reinforced the conflict at the heart of the story. The goal is to create the illusion of complexity, of a complex reality, while structuring that complexity to keep control of the story you're telling.

MIND GAMES

These are some ideas to get you thinking about the consequences of your world-building choices. These are mostly intended to get you started, and maybe making notes, working things out on paper; however, if one of the questions catches your imagination, start writing!

1. What would "seasons" look like to an artificial intelligence? Would it be busy periods vs. quiet periods, or slow lines vs. fast lines, or something else entirely?

2. Imagine a world with an eighty-hour physical day and a twenty-four hour standard clock. How would the two time cycles coincide? What difference would it make, if any?

3. Imagine a world where human beings could eat the animal life but not the plants.

4. Imagine a world where the plants are edible, but also carnivorous and large enough to take human prey. If nothing else, there's a chance that you might eat something that had eaten someone you knew.

5. What would be the consequences of a very fast rotation, one that produced a ten-hour day—approximately five hours of daylight, five hours of night?

6. What would be the consequences of a world so urbanized that "night" is irrelevant as a time of rest—businesses are all open all the time, and somebody, lots of somebodies, are awake and active at all hours?

7. Imagine a society in which your job and eventual status were completely dependent on a series of examinations, starting at the (biological) age of seven. What would it be like to be facing

one of those tests? What would it be like to have failed? To have passed? To have cheated?

8. Imagine a society that grants full civil rights to AIs, but only to certain people. Or to every person and to every level of nonhuman intelligence. Or to all human beings, but not to AIs.

9. Imagine a society that defines "male" as a human being incapable of bearing children. What does that make a person with ovaries, XX chromosomes, breasts, and a vagina who has gone through menopause? How does that redefine femininity—and masculinity? (I'm indebted to M. J. Engh's excellent *Rainbow Man* for the basic premise.)

10. Imagine a society that has finally developed an FTL drive after centuries of settlement at slower-than-light speeds. Would this be a great advance, or would it become a source of tension and conflict?

11. What happens to a society that has based status on hard-to-change physical qualities such as skin color, genetic profile, biological parentage, etc., if it becomes possible to change those factors prenatally? What does this do to the high-status group? To the low-status group?

EXERCISE

Pick one of the ideas above, or choose one of your own, and give some thought to the kind of society and physical setting it might imply. You can combine physical and social questions if you want, but it's generally easier, in a short sketch, to concentrate on one or the other. Then write a short scene in which one character needs something from another character. The second character can cooperate or not, but you'll probably find it easier to create some obstacle preventing the first character from getting what he or she needs. It doesn't matter what the need is (I've seen some rather good sketches in which one character asked another for directions); the object is to get a feel for the physical and social consequences of your choices.

5

CHAPTER

Language and Setting

THE BASIC TOOL OF ALL THE WORLD BUILDING DISCUSSED IN the previous chapter is, of course, language, and words and word choice can become one of your most effective ways of defining your setting. In fact, it's important enough that I think it's worth a separate chapter: most other forms of fiction don't require you to reinvent the language as you go along. I don't mean by this that science fiction writers usually create a full-blown alien language—it's almost impossible to do that well. (The major exception to that statement is J. R. R. Tolkien, himself a linguist able to build on his years of study of Anglo-Saxon and its cognate tongues. Even then, the greater part of his genius was to use words and phrases that could be understood contextually: his readers did not have to become familiar with any of the invented tongues to follow the story.) Instead, I'm talking about something a little more subtle: creating the illusion of a different language, either completely alien or simply removed from our own by time and space, and doing so through the careful use of contemporary language. In general, you have two techniques at your disposal, invented words and real words given new meanings.

In general, I feel that invented terms—completely made-up words—should be used sparingly: on the most basic level, it's really hard to invent new words. You have to have a good ear, and, if you're using more than a few invented words, you need a good sense of grammar and rhythm to make the reader believe that these are all part of the same general language. An obvious solution is to distort an existing word into something that looks and sounds exotic, but this can backfire when the original source is too obvious, or doesn't fit the established culture. For example, Katherine Kurtz, in her Deryni series, used the word *darja* for a drink made from an infusion of leaves. Unfortunately, *darjeeling tea* is pretty common in our own world, and doesn't fit well into a strongly Celtic medieval setting.

Another problem is that invented words, particularly ones attributed to nonhuman characters, are often difficult to pronounce and therefore are difficult for many people to read. This is a classic Catch 22: you the writer are trying to imagine and reproduce sounds made by beings unlike yourself—which almost demands contorted orthography and odd consonant/vowel combinations—but to do so in a way that does not drag your reader out of the flow of the story. Of course every invented word also counts against the strangeness budget, and one of the easiest ways to lose control of a story is to overload it with made-up, unpronounceable words.

That said, it's possible to use invented words to great effect. One of the most common techniques is to pick one or two crucial terms, leave them "untranslated" (trusting the reader to be able either to pronounce them mentally or to skip over the word while recognizing its shape), and to "translate" the rest of the alien terminology into standard English. Larry Niven and Jerry Pournelle use this technique to great effect in The Mote in God's Eye. The aliens known as "Moties" teach the human explorers the important word *fyunch(click)*, which means "friend" and a great deal more, and the implications of which become crucial to the resolution of the plot. Presumably they also teach the humans much more of their language, but other vital Motie concepts are rendered into English—most memorably "Crazy Eddie," the Motie bogeyman that represents for them the cultural baggage that keeps them from solving their problems—and are defined only in English. Not only is this easier on the reader, but it helps Niven and Pournelle create the illusion of a first encounter between aliens and humans. The translation paradoxically reminds us of just how alien these aliens really are.

Along with invented words, one of the most effective ways to create the illusion of a different language is through word choice—

using ordinary (or not so ordinary) English words to mean new things. Obviously, this is most effective when dealing with human beings, so that there's a logical reason for the language to be extrapolated English, but it can work with alien societies as well as long as there is a reason for the words to be translated. This can be something as simple as a line of dialogue saying, "You couldn't pronounce this, so just call me/them/it [blank]." This sounds a little obvious, but in essence it is what Niven and Pournelle did in *The Mote in God's Eye*. A less obvious version of the same technique is to assume that the language you're writing in is the *lingua franca* of your chosen society, and to shape your narrative accordingly. One of the best examples I've ever encountered of this technique is the three Anthony Villiers novels, *Star Well, Masque World*, and *The Thurb Revolution*, written in the late 1960s by the multiple Hugo-winning Alexei Panshin. Here the language is heightened, stylized, a deliberate echo and evocation of late eighteenth- and early nineteenth-century novels of manners—a direct ancestor, in fact, of so-called "mannerpunk" fantasy—and that choice perfectly reflects and creates the social atmosphere in which the stories take place. *Thurb*— a meditative sound made by a member of an alien species known as the Trogs, something like *om* for human Buddhists—is about as foreign as the invented language gets, and it's a highly pronounceable and appropriate-sounding word from a person described as a six-foot-tall furry toad. Instead of piling on invented words, Panshin chooses to make his society seem both alien and futuristic by using a narrative voice relatively uncommon in modern fiction, an omniscient narrator who relates the main story and provides background. That same voice makes it easier for Panshin, in *Star Well*, to introduce some of the less familiar aspects of his world:

> When Villiers rose that morning, he dressed himself and cursed happily at the difficulties of inducing a drapeau to hang correctly behind him without other hands to help. In addition to being decorative, and impressing people, servants had a certain usefulness in delicate and chancy matters like these. Villiers owned an odd and secret gaiety and he enjoyed the exercise of his capacity for wishing bad cess that he might the better spend the rest of the day being his normal good-humored, but reserved, self. . . .
> He chose to be served in the Grand Hall. Villiers followed the old

> dictum, *Live as you dress*. He dressed well. A plump, homely, good-natured girl served him an excellent breakfast. She had left the preserve behind and went to fetch it. It was a living green jelly that grew on rotting vegetation on New Frenchman's Bend, and after an initial unfavorable reaction to it on first encounter, Villiers had decided that he liked the gloppy stuff and ordered it whenever he could. (pp. 23–24)

There is only one non-English word in these paragraphs—*drapeau*—and you don't have to know that it is the French word for "flag" to get a strong impression of just what it is that Villiers is wearing. This drapeau hangs behind its wearer's back and must be adjusted perfectly to make the right impression, a process that is easier with a servant's assistance; this is clearly a very different world from, say, the military spacecraft of *The Mote In God's Eye*. The use of "bad cess," an archaic phrase meaning "wishing ill" or "bad temper," reinforces the impression that this is in some sense an old-fashioned society, one where clothing is dreadfully important, servants are common, and proper behavior is everything. This impression is not contradicted but expanded by the description of the preserve from New Frenchman's Bend. It's clearly something alien and exotic—and moderately disgusting—but the fact that this is one of the items on the menu in this strange space station's best restaurant, and Villiers's reaction to it, also emphasizes the importance of *things* in this society.

Rachel Pollack uses a similar technique to create the alternate future of her novel *Temporary Agency*. By telling the story in the first person, she is able to get in the necessary explanations that carry the reader into her alternate America, and at the same to establish that this world isn't all that different from our own.

> And then, one night, Lisa had some kind of appointment. So Paul stayed home for once and was watching *Slade!*, that cop show on TV where the hero investigates possession for the SDA. In the episode, Slade goes to a Southern town to investigate some mysterious deaths and gets stonewalled by the local sheriff's office. At one point, a woman is running through the swamp, trying to escape a group of Malignant Ones who've taken the form of dogs and cats. She takes refuge in a cabin and bars the door. Inside, she recites the Standard Formula of Recognition. You know, "Ferocious One, I beg you to release me. I know that nothing I have done deserves your Malignant

Intervention." Well, in the story, she gets halfway through the formula when one of the dogs smashes through the door and knocks her to the ground. Then, after they all attack her, they change into the local cops. Shock. Horror. Commercial. (p. 16)

The voice is very clearly the voice of a bright teenager, the main character of the novel, and the overall structure of the *Slade!* episode is one that is all too familiar from series television. The actual plot, on the other hand, is something else entirely: Malignant Ones, the Standard Formula of Recognition, a government agency called the SDA, which you find out earlier stands for the Spiritual Development Agency. Yet because these unfamiliar concepts are slotted into an entirely familiar format, they're at once relatively easy to follow and yet make Pollack's world a distinct and alien place.

Australian writer Terry Dowling uses both invented words and real but uncommon words to create the weird future Australia of his Tom Tyson stories (collected in *Rynosseros*, *Blue Tyson*, and *Twilight Beach*). This technique is probably the most difficult, both for the writer and the reader, but (like so many difficult things) when it's done right it creates a dense and beautiful fiction completely without expository lumps, as in this segment from the short story "Totem" in *Blue Tyson*.

Today beach totems stand along the blazing shores, strange teratoid constructs of bismin, citilo and tri-sephalay, a thousand variants and hybrids as unsettling to see as an unresolved trompe l'oeil or a suspected false perspective or a stairway to nowhere in a half-demolished house. They are called—fittingly enough—Abominations by the tribes, more disturbing than Fosti with its Living Towers (that life project had global acclaim and tribal endorsement at least), more by far than the thousands of belltrees scattered across Australia, left as roadposts beside quiet desert Roads, or set up as tourist novelties on the terraces of the coastal hotels.

The Trale totems seize the eye like a new colour; they stand in the heat of the day like bright stone flowers, or glitter under moon like wet iron or the subtle dozen midnights in an insect's back, inviting apposite names that only art critics and classicists could love: trochars, onagers, spinnerets, magganons—the list goes on, an ambitious attempt to rationalize what simply is. Failed experiments run riot. Abominations. (pp. 213–214)

Dowling's invented words aren't defined in this section, or indeed anywhere in the story, but they echo real words, and by doing so imply their meaning. "Bismin," for example, echoes "bismuth," while "citilo" echoes "chitin"—an association reinforced by the reference to "the subtle dozen midnights in an insect's back." The "real" words that Dowling uses to name the so-called Abominations are equally evocative, and prove to be perfectly descriptive once you know what the words mean. A "trochar," for example, is the instrument used to insert a drainage tube into a body cavity, and the life-form called a trochar draws fluids from the ground and recirculates them. An onager is a kind of catapult, and the onager life-form periodically catapults masses of its waste off into the desert. Spinnerets spin and throw cables. (This is one of the better arguments for developing as wide a vocabulary as possible: the more words you have in your repertoire, the more choices you have for naming alien things and ideas.) None of these words has to be precisely defined; rather, they convey their meaning through implication and context, and the layering of these exotic, uncommon, and unreal words helps Dowling to create Tom Tyson's world as surely as Panshin's formal narration creates the world of Star Well and Pollack's use of acronym and twisted familiarity creates her alternate universe.

What this all really boils down to, though, is the power of names—names for people, places, and things. Obviously—though maybe not so obviously that it isn't worth stating—the names you pick should reinforce the story you're telling. For example, if your story is set in the far future, thousands of years after human beings have left Earth and settled the galaxy, you should have a solid reason for naming your protagonist "Jennifer Smith." (There are such reasons—for example, she's the scion of an incredibly traditional family, the last in a long and illustrious line of Jennifer Smiths—but if you make that choice, the story you're telling should be in some way influenced by the traditionalist mind-set that named her after her ancestors.) If your story is set a few hundred years from now, in a colony on a dead or just-being-terraformed Mars, you probably don't want to invent non-human-sounding place names like "Sheive" or "Ttsma"—which I created by closing my eyes and typing blind—without a solid, and integrally important, reason for them.

The same principles apply to invented objects and technologies, but with the added constraints of the strangeness budget.

People's names—character names—are for me one of the crucial choices in creating a novel, so that's a logical starting point. In fact, they are important enough and the principles involved are universal enough that I think it's worth discussing them in the context of setting as well as characterization. (Of course, if you skipped ahead and read the characterization chapter, you're getting both contexts.) Names tell you things about the society as well as the character; the two sides can't be divorced from each other. I find name choice to be a major decision point for any novel. Several times I've started books, created a protagonist, and then had to change the name in order to bring the character into sharper focus. In the first draft of *Five-Twelfths of Heaven*, the protagonist was named Jensinë, a name that works well enough, but doesn't add anything to the overall feeling of the story. As the society evolved—deeply patriarchal, politically divided, based on a "science" that looked like magic—it became clear to me that this name wasn't working. The protagonist of this novel is a young woman, orphaned, on the verge of developing talents that women simply do not have, so when I saw the name "Silence" (on a list of common Puritan virtue names—I was a graduate student in history at the time), it seemed to sum up the protagonist's situation. Silence was expected, as a woman, to be precisely that, silent, a non-entity, unimportant, but she was none of those things, and in defying her name, she was going to change literally everything. Not that this is ever made explicit in the novel, nor was it a completely conscious decision on my part—*Five-Twelfths* was my second novel—but it implicitly suggests the contradictions that Silence finds in herself and in her world.

I am personally fond of that kind of talismanic or totemic name— you will find characters named Trouble and Fortune in my more recent work—but it's a fairly extreme example of the way character names reinforce the setting. More often, what you'll be aiming for is a suggestion of cultural unity or difference, and an indication of how far in the future your story is set. The main thing, though, will still be the way the name affects *your* perception of the character. Finding the right name for your protagonist(s) is only in part a matter of fitting that name to the setting; there will be times when you will find yourself fitting the setting—and the story itself—to the evocative name.

However, finding good names is surprisingly easy. Resources abound: there are dozens of books intended to help parents name their incipient offspring, dictionaries of names and surnames, odd but useful sources such as concordances (*Proper Names in the Lyrics of the Troubadours* is one that I have used), ethnographic studies, and—best of all—telephone books. The nice thing about baby-name books is that they are absolutely ubiquitous. Nearly every bookstore I have ever been in has at least one, usually under child care, and many carry name books geared to families wanting names from specific ethnic groups or to a non-Anglo market. The latter are particularly worth collecting, because not all of your characters, or your futures, will be descended from contemporary white U.S. society. Names from ethnic groups other than the familiar Anglo- or Celtic-American, especially non-European names, also tend to look and sound "alien" to many of your readers, and can suggest a future no longer dominated by descendants of today's first-world nations. Dictionaries of names and surnames are probably most useful for variant spellings, which help suggest distance from the contemporary world, while oddities like the *Troubadours* provide a pool of common and uncommon names from a shared culture. The most useful "name book" I've ever owned, however, has been my 1984–1985 Manhattan White Pages, which my partner found outside a doctor's office on trash day and brought home for me. (You can get one more easily by ordering it from your phone company, but, since the directory doesn't have to be up-to-date, asking around among friends or offices that do business with New York may turn up one for free.) Manhattan being Manhattan, nearly every ethnic group I could imagine is represented in these pages, and many I rarely think of, which is even better; the book contains 1,653 pages of listings, mostly individual, so I'm in no danger of overusing any one name.

Once you have all these resources, however, you have to figure out how you want to use them. The object, of course, is to find names for your characters, both the central and minor ones, that seem to belong to the society and future that you've created. They should feel in some way related, though that relationship need be no more than one of sound or visual shape. The nearer your setting is to the present, the more likely it is that you can use familiar names and the less likely it is that your imagined culture will have changed so much that you need to emphasize its features by linking the names. Usually I spend a day or two early in the development process of any novel just making a list of names that I think could fit into the book. I divide the list into two columns, one for sur-names and one for personal names, and go through my various resource books, adding to the lists as I go. Sometimes—if there are two competing cultures, for example, or some other groups whose members need to be easily distinguishable from each other—I'll make several name lists, one for each group, but I try to make each one at least one full page long. The selection process is enormous-ly subjective, and can use almost any criteria, but when it's finished, I have a pool of names to draw on for the inevitable moment when I need to call a secondary character something, but don't want to break the narrative flow by stopping and searching all my name books for something that sounds roughly right. The other option, of course, is to simply name those secondary characters with a series of asterisks, and go back at the end of the day and find appropriate names for each one, but frankly I find having a list prepared ahead of time much easier.

Like your people, your imaginary places need names. I find this actually easier than naming the people, not because it is less important—it's equally so—but because the precedents are so clear. If you look at the world around you—perhaps by pulling out a map, as I have just pulled out my AAA map of Kentucky and Tennessee—you'll find that people tend to follow four basic pat-terns in naming towns, and by extension in naming worlds, streets, rivers, and just about anything else in the physical world. First, you can name things after another thing like it—a town after a city "back home," like Memphis or Paris or Portland or Macedonia. Biblical and mythological names are a variation of this principle. Second, you can name things after their physical characteristics, producing towns like Marked Tree (which is actually in Arkansas, but shows up on my map) or Fruithill or Roaring Spring. (Or Cash Point, Beans

Creek, and Skinem, all of which suggest interesting possibilities.) Third, you can name things after their founders or other important people, as in McCains, Russelville, Smiths Grove, Morrison, Kidd's Store, and Kidd's Crossing. Finally, if there is an indigenous population, you can simply adopt their name for the thing in question— Ocoee and Sequatchie are two towns on this map that probably come from Native names.

All these techniques will work for naming places in science fiction as well. There is presently a convention among astronomers that planets, moons, and asteroids within our solar system are given names from mythology, primarily Greek and Roman, and many science fiction writers assume that the same convention will hold for planets outside our system, but you don't have to make that choice. Instead, you can choose the technique that best suits your story. For example, if your protagonist comes from a desert world a long way from the mainstream of galactic society, you are saying very different things about that world and its settlers if you call it "Dustbunny" or "Murchison's Hope" (or "Murchison's Folly")— or Tatooine. Finally, if you're really stuck for names, pick up a map, or walk a few blocks through your own neighborhood, paying attention to the names around you, the streets, stores, local landmarks, even houses, if you live in that kind of neighborhood. The ways that people have named things on this world will work on yours.

You also need names for the invented things—objects, technologies, and so on—that will appear in your story. There are any number of ways of creating them, some of which have been discussed in regard to the authors previously quoted. I tend to break approaches down into four broad methods: conventional names, extrapolation, alternative words, and pure invention. The conventional names are already there for you to use, words whose origins are lost in SF's Golden Age or that were so rapidly adopted by the entire field that they have become universal. These are words like *blaster, communicator, hyperdrive,* and *hyperspace*—or, more recently, *cyberspace, black* ICE, and *the Net.* There's absolutely no reason not to make use of these words and concepts, which are part of the basic toolbox that comes with the decision to write science fiction. However, each one of these terms has accumulated layers of meaning from every other writer that has used them, and those meanings may not suit your purpose, particularly if the object is important to the story. In general, I'd use the conventional terms when they're purely background; something that belongs in the foreground of the story probably needs a more precisely chosen name.

That leaves extrapolation, alternative words, and invention. Extrapolation works very much the way checking maps works for place names. English is evolving around us, and those changes can suggest ways to name the as-yet-imaginary next-stage technologies. For example, suppose I want a name for a new communications system, one that flashes a text message in front of the receiver's vision. (The actual means aren't important for the purposes of the exercise, but you can assume either a transceiver implanted in the eye itself or worn on the person.) This technology would combine the effects of electronic mail, a cellular telephone, and a pager—all of which, by the way, are very new words themselves. I like the way that *electronic mail* and *cellular telephone* have already been shortened to *e-mail* and *cell-phone*, so I'll consider using *mail* or *phone* as a suffix. I don't like *pager*—it's two syllables, for one thing, which makes it a little harder to combine with other words—so I'm going to put that aside for now. The message will appear literally in the blink of an eye—eye movements will be used to control the display—so maybe I'll call it a *blink-phone* or *blink-mail*. Blink-mail works better for me, suggesting speed as well as the mechanics of the transmission and the displayed text. I also think it would be pretty clear just what it is and does, especially in the context of a story. Another possibility is to name your technology after its inventor. I once called a particular kind of weapon a *heylin*, by analogy to Remington or Winchester. As with place names, paying attention to the way words are used—and particularly the ways new words are shortened and worn down in everyday speech—will give you an excellent idea of how to create your own terminology.

I've already discussed both alternate words and pure invention a little bit in connection with Terry Dowling's work. The two are closely related, in that both require a real sensitivity to shape and sound as well as to meaning, and, as with Dowling's writing, they have to be handled carefully, to avoid either expository lumps or reader overload. Alternative words are, very simply, archaic or unfamiliar words for more familiar terms, and, reasonably enough, one of the best sources for them is the thesaurus. Words labeled archaic or obsolete may be exactly the ones you need to evoke a sense of both the familiar and the alien. This is one of the cases in which new is less effective than old, however: I have found that my 1946 edition of *Roget's International Thesaurus*, in which *aircraft, aeronautics,* and *aeronaut* are all late additions, contains a number of synonyms that are no longer in current usage. Perversely, these old words are ripe for reuse in a futuristic setting.

Another source of alternative words is foreign languages, particularly if those languages evoke the culture you're trying to create. Over the years, I've collected a number of travelers' phrase books and student dictionaries in languages ranging from Korean and Japanese to Russian and Swahili, all of which have given me ideas for alternative words. For example, in my novel *Dreamships*, in which the dominant cultures are non-European, I was looking for an alternative word for the motorbike driven by one of the characters. I wanted something that would sound unfamiliar but at the same time be easily recognizable, and turned to my phrase books for inspiration. There was nothing in the Japanese phrase book that I wanted to use, and Korean simply didn't have the right sound; however, the onomatopoeic Swahili word for motorcycle, *pikipiki*, was close to what I wanted. It didn't quite fit the other invented words I was using, however, so I broke it in half and recombined it with my original thought to produce a *piki-bike*. I derived the honorifics *bi'* and *ba'* (used like Ms. and Mr.) from an abbreviation for *binti* (meaning Miss), in the same phrase book.

Invented words can be as elaborate and evocative as Dowling's "bismin" and "citilo" or as simple as the old standby, "blaster." "Blaster" is, in fact, a classic example of one of the simplest invented forms in English, taking a useful verb and adding the suffix *er* to turn it into a noun. It's extremely common in science fiction—Andre Norton's favorite invented handgun, the "Gauss needler," for example, or "communicator"—and in real life, with words like *computer, toaster,* or *writer.* Another technique (at least for typists) is to collect interesting typos—sometimes a slip of the finger will produce an interesting recasting of an ordinary word. (For example, in the previous sentence, I originally wrote "tyists." I don't know what it would mean, but it will certainly go on my list of possible words.) I actually do keep a list of "good" typos, and check it when I'm really stumped for ideas. Also for typists is my old standby, typing blind, or, as a friend once called it, typing in tongues. I use this mostly for alien names, ID numbers, and computer codes, or occasionally for acronyms or nonessential jargon. The technique is simple: place your hands on the keyboard, close your eyes, and type. The results usually need editing, but it's a place to start when you need something fast.

I've spent this much time on words because they are the basic tool you'll use to recreate on the page the worlds you've imagined. All the work you've put in on the physical and social setting can easily be spoiled by trite and conventional terms; familiar settings can gain new life through a highly imagined language. Spending time to try on new terms, to find exactly the right word instead of the conventional image, to make the names and the terminology seem to flow from the same imagined culture, will pay off for you. Your worlds, and your characters acting in those worlds, will seem more real, more believable, and your story will be the better for it.

MIND GAMES

These are ideas to ponder and lists to collect/create more than they are actual writing exercises; I'm thinking of them as springboards for your imagination (or crowbars for your brain) rather than as exercises that will produce a finished product. However, all of them are things that I do for nearly every novel I write, and the lists that they produce become part of my reference package for that novel.

1. Sit down with one or more baby-name books, or with the telephone directory, and compile a list of at least forty names that you think "go together." Start with Z and go backwards through the book until you reach A; don't think too much about the results, but concentrate on collecting them. When you've finished, put the list into a form in which you can see all the names at once, and study them. What makes them similar? Did you pick them for sound or shape, or ethnic group, or something else? What kind of a culture would produce this group of people?

2. Get your thesaurus (and this really is one of the things you should own, though not necessarily for the reasons your English teacher told you) and make a list of possible alternative words for the following concepts: gun, policeman, flying machine, network, spaceship, monarch, salesman. Remember, you don't want direct synonyms, but words that you can use to imply something similar yet very different.

3. If you're a typist, start collecting your mistakes. Some of them—simple transpositions like "beofre" for "before"—probably won't be much use, but you may find that perfect word for your latest technological wonder iurking in the keyboard.

6

CHAPTER

Peopling Your Worlds

TO TALK ABOUT CHARACTER IS TO TALK ABOUT DESIRE AND need—what the people in your story want or need badly enough to make the events happen. As with your setting, the basic "what if" sets boundaries on what it is your characters want by defining the parameters of the story. A story in which the "what if" is, say, the development of the first faster-than-light drive system is unlikely to be peopled with characters whose main desire is to resolve a love affair—unless that love affair is somehow intimately connected to the development of the new drive. On the other hand, the electronic cash idea, which carries with it the idea of a constant conflict between face value and real value, might well call for characters whose greatest need is to find someone they can trust, and thus put a love affair very much at the center of the story.

A crucial corollary to this idea is that the desire must be something concrete. To borrow from the theater, a character's objective has to be something *playable*—it has to be something that an actor could convey, not something that you as the writer have to explain to your readers. In the real world, people don't go around declaring that their life's ambition is to do something worthwhile (and, human nature being what it is, when we do meet people like that, we tend to dismiss them as unrealistic); you're more likely to hear people say that they want to raise a child, or find a cure for AIDS, or even something relatively small and personal like write a novel or sail around the world. In other words, "being a hero" is a worthy goal, but it's hard to bring that down to something that an individual could realistically do. On the other hand, "rescuing the princess" is something much more specific—and it's worth remembering that when we first meet Luke Skywalker, his main desire is to get off Tatooine. In some ways, "rescuing the princess" is just a particularly spectacular way of achieving that first goal—as it is also a concrete way of "becoming a hero."

Once you've figured out what it is your character wants, and how that fits with your "what if," you're faced with two pairs of corollary questions. The first is, what will your character do to achieve that goal—and what *won't* that character do? Classic examples are the pacifist who would rather die than kill another human being, or the hard-boiled detective—Sam Spade is, I believe, the original, or at least the classic version—who would let the woman he loves go to prison, or even hang, rather than betray his code of honor. In each of these cases, the character comes up against something that is fundamental to his or her sense of self and must either betray that sense of self or lose something that is equally important. That brings us to the second of the corollary pairs: what is at stake if your character fails—or succeeds? In classic science fiction, the stakes can be very high indeed. In the final volume of James Blish's *Cities in Flight*, for example, at stake is, literally, the universe itself. The choice for the characters should be correspondingly difficult and drastic. (In *Cities in Flight*, the characters must ultimately choose between their own continued existence and the recreation of the universe: you can't get much bigger than that.) The answers to these questions—what your main character wants, what he or she will and won't do to get it, and the overall stakes—form the emotional core of your story.

Keeping these questions in mind will also help avoid another of the major pitfalls for all writers, that of the unearned ending. This is another idea that I have borrowed from theatrical writing, but one that has proved really useful to me as a novelist. In essence, this is that idea that a character's success or failure should be *earned*—that is, it should grow organically out of the character's previous decisions and actions. In other words, if you wanted a version of *The Maltese Falcon* in which Sam Spade and Bridget O'Shaughnessy live (un)happily ever after (instead of his sending her to certain prison and possible hanging for the murder of Spade's partner), you couldn't simply keep the story intact but have him suddenly melt in response to her last appeal. After all, every other time that Spade was faced with a choice between his principles and another person, he chose his principles—Hammett establishes early in the novel that the one thing Spade will not do is compromise his personal vision of honor, and reinforces the point repeatedly. It would be impossible to believe that Spade would make all those other sacrifices worthless by throwing his honor to the winds, merely for Bridget O'Shaughnessy. Instead, you would have to prepare your readers for this change of heart by showing Spade willing to compromise on larger and larger issues in order to make his ultimate choice of O'Shaughnessy over honor believable—an earned ending. In fact, Hammett did such a good job of creating this character, and setting up the conflict between honor and desire, that it has become something of a cliché. A writer now would have to go to a similar effort to set up a character who would betray his principles for another person—as director Ridley Scott did in the movie *Bladerunner*. (The original novel, *Do Androids Dream of Electric Sheep?* by Philip K. Dick, was structured to emphasize different aspects of the question of what it means to be human.)

It's worth contrasting the two stories and the two views of the dedicated detective as examples of these principles at work. In both, we're introduced to a detective figure who seems to want only to be left alone to do his job. As the story progresses, however, it becomes clear that Sam Spade's private eye and Deckard's bladerunner (the person responsible for hunting down and killing renegade androids) want, more than anything, to keep their personal honor intact in a world that demands far too much compromise. Both men are tempted to bend their principles in order to help a person whom they find attractive: Spade to help O'Shaughnessy, Deckard to help the android Rachel. However, in *The Maltese Falcon*, every incident serves to reinforce and reaffirm Spade's determination to catch the killer of his partner (a man he didn't particularly like, and in fact was cuckolding). In *Bladerunner*, however, every incident is constructed to force Deckard to question the rightness of his choices, and in the end, although he kills the rene-gade androids who have already killed their creator, he runs away with Rachel—steals her, according to his society—in a probably futile attempt to prolong her life. Even the points of view are cho-sen to reinforce these endings: *The Maltese Falcon* is told entirely from Spade's perspective, in very tight third person, while *Bladerunner* shows scenes from multiple points of view, and particularly from the renegades' perspective, so that the viewer in some sense knows more than Deckard does and therefore is prepared for his eventual choices. The endings are exactly opposite, but both are fully earned.

Of course, it can be hard to think of character in such abstract terms, at least in the early stages of imagining a project. (Personally, I find it almost impossible, which is why I tend to think about set-tings first.) I think most of us start with an image, or a flash of inspi-ration—this is one of the reasons so many writers talk about a char-acter "popping into their heads" or "walking into the story." Nevertheless, it's important to keep those three issues—what the characters want, what they will do to get it, and what's at stake if they fail—in mind as you work on the concrete questions that follow.

The main thing that a writer needs to do in creating a protagonist is to invent someone your readers can care about. They don't have to like your protagonist, though it's harder to keep their interest if they don't, but they do have to care what happens to him or her, and care enough to keep reading until the end of the book. This means that *you* should care about your protagonist, too—and the more you care about a character, the more likely it is that that character should be your protagonist. Occasionally, I read stories in which the ostensible protagonist exists only to be a lens through which the reader perceives a more interesting secondary character. Sometimes this works, but more often it's just a way of avoiding engaging fully with that main character. When the technique does work, it's usually because the viewing character is both interesting in his or her own right, and because you need the viewing charac-ter's perceptions to interpret the secondary character's behavior for the reader. Dr. Watson and Sherlock Holmes are classic examples of the technique (let's face it, Holmes would be unbearable if he was the only point of view character), but Poul Anderson used it to similar effect in his Nick van Rijn stories. In these, van Rijn is an overbearing, obnoxious senior merchant—who nonetheless is the smartest man around when it comes to resolving problems with inscrutable aliens. He would be unbearable as a point of view character—what readers want to imagine themselves as overbearing and obnoxious?—and Anderson wisely pairs him with viewpoint characters who are generally decent people, the kind of people most readers (and writers) would like to be. These characters are usually wrong, and van Rijn is usually right, but they are wrong for reasons that anyone can understand.

Eleanor Arneson uses a variation of the technique in *Ring of Swords*. In many ways, the protagonist of the novel is the human Nicholas Saunders, a former prisoner-of-war who has not merely joined the enemy aliens but has become the lover of one of their generals. Indeed he is one of the point of view characters. However, in order fully to understand his situation, and to resolve both the plot and the characters' problems, a second, outside point of view is required, and Arneson introduces Anna Perez, a xenobiologist accidentally caught up in the high politics. Perez's uncertainties and her analysis of the situation help the reader to understand Saunders's choices, good and bad.

Another important factor—which is not unique to SF, though SF makes it more explicit than most forms—is that your protagonist has to be intimately involved with the story's "what if." Even if the "what if" is apparently just an obstacle interfering with the protagonist's real desire, it has to be resolved in order for the protagonist to reach his or her goal. Generally, though, it's better (and easier for both writer and readers) to use the "what if" to help define the protagonist's desires. To go back to the examples introduced in Chapter 2, the protagonist of a story based on the galleys idea would almost certainly need to be connected to those ships. That protagonist could be a prisoner, desperate to escape or simply to survive, or an officer, who wants to keep the ship intact through its period of service—or who has come to doubt the wisdom and/or the morality of the system. It could be one of the architects, either of the ships or of the penal system (or both), who has to confront the consequences of those choices. It could also be a prisoner's or an officer's spouse, whose life is bounded and defined by the movement of the ship that holds his or her partner. Whichever alternative you choose, the galleys need to be at the center of the characters' needs—or you need to consider finding a different "what if." The same is true of the electronic cash idea: your characters need to have some real connection to it. They could be creators of the currency, or forgers of it, or they could need electronic cash for some other purpose. Maybe it's more stable than any other form, or more volatile, and they need to manipulate that market in some way. Or maybe acquiring an electronic cash account would prove that one or more characters could trust the others. . . . The possibilities are endless, and the only limits are imposed by your original "what if."

Once you've got a basic idea of the main characters, however, you need to flesh out the details—who they are, where they come from, and what they're doing in this story. This, like world building, is largely a matter of asking yourself questions, and then pushing those answers as far as you choose to take them. The process is a little different but the goal is the same: to get you thinking about the factors that go into interesting and realistic characters.

One way to begin is to think of an attribute—a skill, a habit, an emotional trait—that you have, or that you wish you had, or that you admire or fear in someone else, or even that you fear you might have. It could be anything: mechanical aptitude (I think of a friend who collects and restores old Volkswagens), a chronic illness, a knack for picking up new languages, an explosive temper, or the ability to switch off one's emotions under stress. Play with the trait—exaggerate it, push it to unreasonable extremes, pare it down to little more than a quirk, but explore what it would be like to put that at the center of your character. How does it work with your "what if"? Does it reinforce your character's involvement in your story, or does it tend to push him or her away from events? If the latter, how could you get the person involved with the "what if" without losing the characteristic's force? For example, an explosive temper could fit rather well with the galley idea: it provides a reason for the character to be on one of the galleys—he's been incarcerated for something he did in anger—and it sets up the possibility of an immediate conflict. This character will have to learn to control his temper, or he won't survive his time on the galley. A chronic illness is a less obvious match with that idea—though, again, a character with certain kinds of chronic illness would be presented with unique challenges, and automatic conflict, in this world—but could fit extremely well with the electronic cash idea. The illness provides a need for money—to pay for treatment, to leave to dependents, simply to live in comfort—that sets up the need to manipulate the cash system; it could also, depending on the nature of the disease, add to the issues of trust and face vs. real value. The goal is to find a core of the character that you want to explore and that supports and is supported by your "what if."

Then you can move on to what I think of as the basic biography, starting with the facts you'd find on someone's driver's license. The name is often the first thing you think of wanting to know about a character, though I've found that it's easier for me to wait until I know more about the character before settling on a full name. Other people, though, start with a name, and use those associations as a springboard into developing the character. I'm not talking (necessarily) about the meanings of names that you see in "name your baby" books—those can easily lead to heavy-handed symbolism—but about the emotions and images a particular name evokes for you. One way of getting going on an idea is to thumb through a book of names and stop at random to see what name appears—or, like my great-grandmother, open a Bible and point. The odds are that you won't find something you like that way, but each rejected name will help you define what you are looking for.

On the other hand, "address" is something most people don't think about very much, and that's too bad. Knowing a little bit about where your characters live can be very helpful in defining who they are as people. I'm not talking about a complete street or mailing address, of course, though inventing that could be as evocative as looking for names, but rather about what kind of environment your characters have chosen or are forced to live in. After all, the person who lives in a mobile home is likely to be different from the person who lives in a mansion, if only in terms of resources. So another good question to ask is in just what sort of place do your characters live? Does your space freighter captain live on her ship, or does she keep a one-room apartment in the space station where she docks most often—or does she live with a succession of men on the various worlds she visits? Does the teacher on your frontier world live in his own house, or does he board with the family of one of his students, as frontier teachers did in our own past? Is this a comfortable place to live—and remember, definitions of comfort may vary according to conditions. A character in the decaying cities typical of cyberpunk might count himself rich to have two rooms in a secure building, while the same two secure rooms might be miserable poverty to a character on an expanding frontier world. Did your characters choose this place, or did they have no other options?

The next item on a driver's license (on mine, anyway) is gender. In our society, at least, this is such a basic factor in our responses to a person that the choice of a character's gender often gets made on a subconscious level. A character arrives in your brain as male or female (or, given that this is SF, something else), and that choice cannot, and often should not, be shaken. One of the great advantages of science fiction as a genre is that gender and gender roles are defined by the writer, so that combinations that would be unthinkable or at best unlikely in our own society—male mothers, for example, or female serial killers—are more easily achieved. On a less extreme level, it is possible in SF to assume the basic competence of a character regardless of gender, and not have to spend as much time justifying a nontraditional choice.

Sometimes, however, a character appears as a type, a person defined by a job or some other role, which may or may not contain an obvious choice of gender. You may well have some idea of whether this character is a man or a woman (or whatever), but not be committed to the choice yet. In that case, it's not a bad idea to spend a few minutes imagining the character as a different gender. Most of the time, you'll probably end up reaffirming your original choice, but even if you do it's frequently helpful to come to a conscious understanding of why you made that choice in the first place. Also, if you find yourself always writing characters of one gender, you should try writing someone of the opposite gender, even if it's just a brief sketch or two. After all, if you can't imagine yourself in the head of a man (or a woman), how are you ever going to imagine yourself inside the head of someone who isn't human at all?

As a further note on gender and characters, I discovered some time ago that one of the easiest ways to achieve a futuristic society was to make both my writing and the societies it described as gender-blind as possible. In other words, since English requires you to attach a gender—even the neuter "it"—to people as they are described, I wanted to make sure that women were doing the so-called nontraditional jobs in the backgrounds of my stories. Of course, in the process, I ran up against my own biases: I caught myself giving all the jobs I liked to female characters, which unbalanced the invented societies in a whole new way. To correct this bad habit without spending too much time trying to keep count of who'd been what most recently, I resorted to the random coin-flip. I decided in advance that heads would be female, tails male, and for each minor character that appeared, I flipped a coin. (For *Shadow Man*, in which 25 percent of the characters had to belong to one of three intersexual genders, I rolled twelve-sided dice to make sure I kept the numbers right.) If you couple this kind of strictly random choice with gender-neutral language—*parent* instead of *mother* or *father*, *sibling* instead of *brother* or *sister*, OK, *people*, instead of *All right, men*, and so on—you can achieve a subtly foreign effect without either confusing your readers or hitting them over the head. Of course, this doesn't work if you're writing about a society that *does* have distinct gender roles. You can use the same method to ensure that any other random division in your society appears in the proper proportion. If 10 percent of your population is telepathic, for example, rolling dice or using some other genuinely random method each time a new character is mentioned will help keep the percentages where you wanted them.

Age is the next important statistic on my license, and, like name and address, it's one that I don't like to fix too specifically too early. On the other hand, I do need to know whether a character is young or old—and indeed, what that society considers young and old. Age, after all, does set some limits on how much (or how little) your characters could realistically be expected to have done in their lives. It's hard to believe in a twenty-year-old doctor or senior naval captain, or a fifty-year-old beginning clerk typist, unless you're prepared to explain why your characters or your society deviates so strongly from our norms. And you can deviate, of course. Geoff Ryman's brilliant The Child Garden presents a population in which, because everyone is educated by virus, children know everything they need to know to function in society by the age of seven or eight. (This is a good thing, as one of the side effects of the virus is to kill its carriers by the time they're thirty.)

After age come the rough details of appearance: height, weight, skin, hair and eye color (the last four unspecified, but reasonably clear from the photo). As with names, you're looking for characteristics that are personally evocative, not symbolic. (A "cruel mouth" is not only a cliché, but also a meaningless description.) It may be helpful to think in general terms: ask yourself if your character is tall or short, rather than worrying about precise heights; interestingly ugly or ravishingly gorgeous, instead of committing yourself immediately to a set of features. On the other hand, if you find you know the answers to these questions right away, jot them down. Better still, write a short paragraph or two describing the character or characters, and save it with the rest of your notes. You probably won't have occasion to use the entire sketch, but you may find one or two lines or images that you can use in the final draft of your story. (I once wrote a long, loving description of a secondary character, filed it with the rest of the notes and sketches for a story, and extracted from it a single phrase—"[blue] eyes as lightless as pooled ink"—which remains in the novel to this day.) Finally, does your character look pretty much like everyone else in the story, or different from them?

The next question I ask myself is usually what the character does, either as a job, or as the central focus of his or her life. In most of my work, the two are one and the same, and that central focus is always something that connects the character to the story's "what if." In Dreamships, for example, Reverdy Jian is a pilot who works with FTL systems and the near-AI constructs that human beings must employ to take ships through hyperspace. The job puts her in day-to-day contact with the most complex computer programs, something that is vital both to the plot and to the central question of what is, and isn't, true AI. In Burning Bright, Quinn Lioe is a pilot, too, but she is also a designer of episodes within the Game that dominates human culture, and the conflict between the two identities throws her into the center of the story. Ideally, your "what if" should make your characters' profession and/or avocation obvious. In the galley idea, for example, your characters should probably have some strong connection to the ships themselves, while the electronic cash idea seems to demand some reason for the characters to be familiar with computers and finances.

Once that central piece is in place, it's time to ask more questions. If the thing the characters do isn't their job, then what do they do to make ends meet? Do they like their work, or is it just a day job? (How do their employers feel about their work?) Are they part of a specific class or caste that performs that job or avocation? Are there special requirements—physical size and strength, gender or race or ethnic group, psychic abilities, educational levels, and so on—that your character must seem to meet? Are there any special requirements—talent, secret knowledge, better education than average—to do that job well? Do the characters' jobs affect their bodies? Basketball players, for example, need to be tall, contortionists need flexible joints, and pilots need excellent eyesight; guitarists develop calluses on their fingers and swimmers develop massive back and shoulder muscles. Can someone look at your character's body and tell what he or she does? Do your characters' bodies have to be modified for them to do their jobs? (If so, how do your characters feel about it—other people as well as your protagonist?) A final question to ask yourself: what will your character do for a living after your story ends?

Once you've made some basic decisions about your characters, you can start connecting them to the rest of your fictional universe. I tend to go from the information on a driver's license to the information you might get from a census form. In other words, is your character single, married or partnered, dating (seriously or not), celibate, divorced, widowed? What's his ethnic group? Her religion? Are the main characters part of the majority, or in a minority, and does that matter? Do they live alone, or with other people; if they live with others, who are those people? Do they have children, or other people dependent on them? Do they have some other kind of dependent? In a society in which machine intelligence is a contested issue, an artificial intelligence might function as a dependent, needing a human guardian to interact with human society. (Or— and I'm indebted to the GURPS *Space* book for this idea—your character might have custody of an egg, either the conventional, hard-shelled variety or the less familiar germ plasm, or even of a fertilized embryo.) If your characters have this kind of responsibility, how do they handle it? Do they even want it? What about money? Are they struggling, comfortable, well-off—can they afford to experience the events of your story, or will they have to struggle for money as well as for the solution to their problems? Are they native to where they live, or immigrants, and does it matter? Are they citizens, or not?

Of course, what all of these questions are getting at is the ways in which your characters are connected to each other and to the world around them, and that brings up the question of the most intimate connections of all, those of family. For years, it's been something of a cliché that science fiction heroes existed in a figurative as well as literal vacuum; they were all only children who were uncommitted to any personal relationships and whose parents were dead. While this has always been something of an exaggeration (even Kimball Kinneson, hero of E. E. "Doc" Smith's classic space operas, acquired a wife and children during his adventures), nonetheless the rugged individual is still the template for many SF protagonists. This is not to say that every protagonist should come complete with multiple generations of relatives, but it is always worth thinking about your characters' family backgrounds. Even if you never make these backgrounds explicit, a person who has deliberately broken with her family is likely to behave differently in her other relationships than someone who has always stayed on good terms with every member of his extended clan. Knowing these things about your characters can give you insights into how they might deal with other situations.

To begin with, how do your characters define a family? Is it just biological relatedness, or does it include close friendships, unmarried lovers, and/or same-sex partnerships? Does your characters' definition coincide with their society's, and if it doesn't, how much difficulty does that cause them? Are their parents living? What about grandparents, great-grandparents, and other older generations? (You could do something really interesting with a character whose most distant known ancestor was somehow preserved, perhaps as a computer copy of his or her memories, and present to meddle in the family's business.) How about same-generation relatives—siblings and cousins—or relatives in the parents' generation? Are there children, nieces, nephews, younger-generation cousins? How extended is the family? Do your characters stop the family with first cousins, or do they keep track of complicated degrees of consanguinity? (The latter might be important in preventing genetic problems in a relatively small population, like a recently settled colony, space station, or single starship.) Are your characters in constant contact with their kin, deeply involved in their lives, do they avoid them, or is the relationship something in between those extremes? Do they care about their family connections, or are they casual about them? Do they get anything—status (low or high), money, introductions, and so on—from being part of their family?

The answers to these questions help to define the society in which your story takes place. If you've done your world building first, you need to be aware of what your choices demand from your society, and adjust either your society or your characters to avoid unhelpful contradictions. If, for example, you've decided that family relationships are extremely important not just to your main characters but to everyone, at the very least you imply a society that is capable of keeping track of complex census data, and you need to be sure that such a mechanism exists in your imagined world, whether it be computerized data banks or specially trained individuals. You might also want to be sure that there is, or was in the past, a reason for the society's concern with kinship. This could be genuine need (a small population with a reason to fear genetic defects), preference (groups wishing to maintain an ethnic identity or to retain family property), or prejudice (the desire to preserve a group's perceived superior traits), or something else, but a decision like that is likely to have further ramifications for your society. Of course, as always, some contradictions actually add to the illusion of reality. If this kinship-obsessed society no longer has any reason to be so aware of these relationships—if the population has grown enough to make genetic drift less of a problem, or if the things being preserved are no longer relevant—then the contradiction between what society wants and what society may actually need becomes a possible source of conflict for the story. If you've begun with character, then you've set some guidelines that your world building should support. If, for example, you've decided that your main character was born from a mechanical womb, bypassing family altogether, then you've not only established a fairly high level of technology for your world, but you've implied either a reason for avoiding the usual process of gestation and birth or a character exceptional in his or her society.

At this point, you may find that you've created a character who is remarkably similar to yourself. On one level, this is unavoidable and even desirable—there will always be a little bit of yourself in all your characters, some spark of empathy that lets you understand *why* even the antagonists behave as they do—but too great a similarity can cause difficulties. If you identify too completely with a character—if your protagonist *is* you—you risk losing the emotional distance you need to tell the story fairly, including a character's mistakes and weaknesses as well as his or her strengths.

How can you achieve this distance? The obvious way is to make sure your character is different from you, and in some significant ways. One common method is to make sure the character looks different from you. Make him or her tall, if you're short, fat (or at least full-figured) if you're thin, strikingly gorgeous or fascinatingly ugly if you're ordinary-looking—but again, be careful of wish-fulfillment descriptions. One of the biggest visual clichés in science fiction is the green-eyed redhead (a cover artist of my acquaintance once complained that she was running out of ways to make all the redheads look different). Descriptions that draw from reality, and not just the buffed and sculpted reality of movie stars, will serve you better in the long run than the stereotypes. Think about what "green" eyes actually look like: it's not generally a shade like emerald (unless the person is wearing colored contacts) but something closer to agate, a brownish, yellow-toned green not very different from the color usually described as hazel. Looking at real people and trying to describe them accurately, without using clichés, is a very good exercise, and it can help you create more believable characters. Suzy McKee Charnas has talked about making the conscious decision to describe the characters in *Motherlines* (all women) as she saw real women in the world around her, rather than relying on the standard nondescriptions she had inherited from an older school of writing. Immediately after the book was published—in 1978—she says the most frequent comment she received was "but why did you make them all so ugly?" In reading the novel now, however, I'm struck by the realism of her descriptions, and by the ways that she uses observation of real people to make the various characters completely individual. While this story has a clear feminist moral (which I should probably make explicit nonetheless: Charnas was one of the first group of SF writers, feminists all, to treat women as worthy of observation, and those observations did not always jibe with the conventional beliefs about women), it is also a reminder that only by really looking at people will you be able to write about them. You may not always produce conventional "beauty," but you're likely to come up with something more interesting.

Sometimes something that is relatively small can be a very powerful tool for separating yourself from your characters. For example, I have found that food habits and choices work well for me, possibly because I enjoy cooking and eating. It is helpful to me, when I'm trying to create characters that can take on a life of their own, to think about what they habitually eat, regardless of whether or not I would like it. This also involves thinking about the setting, what foods are available, cheap, expensive, and so on, but since I generally do most of that work before I start working seriously on character, it's relatively easy for me. Clothing style could work in a similar way, as could sports preferences, or anything else that is personally evocative.

Another, and perhaps more powerful, method for separating yourself from your protagonist is to change something really big— to write about someone whose race, gender, religion, or sexual preference is different from your own. The advantage to this is that it immediately makes you write outside yourself, to write from observation as well as imagination. Your character is visibly and obviously not yourself; you are automatically freed from paralyzing self-consciousness—the feeling that everyone will know you're talking about yourself and your own life. Even though you identify with your characters on one level, on another you have already taken a step back from them. It helps you think of the character first, rather than of your personal reactions, which may or may not be appropriate. It also pushes you to widen your own scope as a writer, to learn to create a broad range of characters.

There are, of course, drawbacks to writing someone so different from yourself, not least of which is the simple fact that it's hard work. It involves learning as much as you can about the lives of the group you've decided to write about, and that entails listening carefully to be sure you're hearing the people themselves and not what you or the dominant group think about these people. It means reading books by members of the group, both books about being a member of that group and books that are ostensibly about something else but are inevitably affected by that experience. It means talking to your friends who are part of that group, and maybe to their friends as well; it means listening carefully to what all these people tell you, and trying to catch the emotional core of their lives. I've found that it's often a matter of hearing the personal consequences of something I knew only as a fact—like the time a male friend was talking, half laughing, half rueful, about spending all of his junior high school years holding his books in front of his crotch and hoping his arms were long enough. Now, I knew adolescent males got erections at the most inappropriate moments, and practically without cause, but I hadn't really thought much about what it would be like to live with that—and it suggests to me a way in which men's experience of their bodies is generally somewhat different from women's. I had a similar revelation after walking through a downtown area with another male friend, a fellow writer this time. Three men were hanging out on the corner, too heavily dressed for the (warm) weather, and all of them were carrying heavy walking sticks. I found them potentially threatening and insisted we cross the street to avoid them. Discussing it, both my friend and I were struck by our very different awareness of potential threat (these guys hadn't actually *done* anything, or even said anything) and of our underlying assumptions about what would happen if there was trouble. I had assumed, instinctively and not entirely with cause, that we would be beaten and would need to run away; he had assumed, also instinctively, and not entirely without reason, that we could fight back successfully. Much of the difference was, I think, cultural, but it suggested another way to look at violence. Obviously, these are not universal characteristics of gender—my sister the black belt reacts very differently to physical threat, and I know plenty of men who are as aware of potential danger as I am— but it took me outside of my own assumptions.

Getting to the emotional core isn't easy when you're writing about people whose cultures and lives you share, and when you compound the difficulty by needing to learn basic facts (and unlearn old assumptions), you increase the risk of failure. If you are working with issues that are contested in our own world—race, gender, ethnic identity, religious beliefs, and sexual habits and preferences are only a few of the possible minefields—the stakes get very high, and it's easy to misjudge. The biggest danger, I think, in writing about groups that you consider Other is in treating them as objects when your story demands that you treat them as subjects. For example, I recently read an interview in which a mystery writer discussed her decision to make her protagonist a lesbian in order to write about a friendship and professional partnership between a man and a woman in which sexual tension played no part. Aside from any practical considerations (Would the partner really be less likely to be attracted to a lesbian than to a straight woman? Are straight men and women really incapable of being friends?), this character's lesbianism wasn't a sexuality, it was an absence of heterosexuality. The author's interest was not in the character as a lesbian, but as a not-heterosexual, so that she could avoid dealing with a problem that is of primary relevance to heterosexual characters. On the other hand, taking the chance—and it can be a big one—not only stretches you as a writer but offers you the opportunity to view the world from new perspectives. Can you think of better practice for, say, inventing aliens?

MIND GAMES

1. Collect faces. I personally find this very evocative, and the wall beside my desk is covered with pictures cut from magazines

and newspapers, postcards, photos, and the occasional painting or drawing. Some of them were chosen because I wanted to have a physical reference for a character or a story, and some I just like, but I find that having a wide variety of faces immediately visible above my desk forces me to write more honestly about appearance.

For a quick start, pick a photo of a person and describe him or her. Really look at the picture, and see if you can find a detail you've never noticed before about anyone. Have you ever seen it mentioned in a book? Can you use it in a way that makes it sound as though it's never been mentioned before? (Beware of overwriting here! You're not aiming for purple prose, but for some simple thing—chipped nail polish, the way someone's hairline recedes, or the extra ring of color in someone's iris—that you can use to make the description seem fresh.)

2. Make a list of ten characteristics that you like: that you approve of, or would like to have, or admire in other people. These can be as general as "competence" or as specific as "the ability to write Unix." Now make a list of ten characteristics that you dislike, whether in yourself or in other people. As before, these can be really general ("bigotry") or really specific ("nail biting").

   Pick one characteristic from each list—you can pick the least personally offensive of the dislikes, but make sure it's something you really do dislike—and imagine a character who has both of them. How do the two interact? Is this character at odds with herself, or do the two characteristics dovetail better than you would have expected? Is the character trying to overcome the flaw you picked from the dislikes column—or is he trying to get rid of the characteristic you picked from the likes?

   You can also do this in a more random fashion by cutting each list into individual entries, and drawing one from the likes and one from the dislikes. Or you could even mix them all together and draw from the entire pool—you run the risk of getting two disliked characteristics in exchange for the chance of getting two characteristics you like.

3. If you did the "personals" exercise in Chapter 2, you might try that again, this time trying to imagine the person who placed the randomly chosen ad. Is he like the ad, or is she lying wildly?

4. Jot down the events of your character's average day. You can be as detailed as you want, but be sure to get all of the basic events. Then pick an interesting event—it can be part of the normal day, or a break with the routine—and sketch it as a brief scene. How does your character interact with his or her world?

5. Troubleshooting: There are some studies (which I encountered when they were cited in Carol Tavris's *The Mismeasure of Woman*) that suggest that when people talk of two items they tend to define one in terms of the other—A and not-A—but when talking of three or more items will find separate adjectives to describe each one—A, B, and C. This is particularly noticeable in parents' descriptions of their children. Parents of two children tended to describe their children in terms of each other— *Jane is athletic, Steve isn't athletic*—while parents of three children gave each child an individual adjective—*Jane is athletic, Steve is sociable, Dell is smart*. I think there's a tendency for writers to do this to their characters as well, particularly when one gets involved with a particularly attractive protagonist. (And protagonists tend to be attractive, or they wouldn't be protagonists.) It's all-too easy to define the antagonist or even the secondary protagonist by comparison to the protagonist: *my protagonist is incredibly deft on the Net; my antagonist /secondary protagonist is clueless about computers*. This leads to a character who looks even flatter by comparison to your protagonist, who, after all, is the character who interested you most in the story in the first place, and on whom, justifiably, you've spent most of your creative efforts.

A very useful self-check, especially when you're dealing with two characters who have to be equally strong and interesting to preserve the balance of the story, is to make sure you have descriptions of each one that don't rely on the other's presence. Here are some exercises to help you get to that point:

1. Make a list of adjectives that describe your primary character, the one you're not having trouble with. Do the same for the secondary character. Do it quickly, trusting your instincts, and don't worry about using shorthand that means something to you and not to anybody else—you'll have plenty of chances to expand and define those phrases later in your actual writing, but this is really just for you. Now, how many of those adjectives form complementary pairs? Is there one pair of oppositions that defines the relationship between the characters? (This is more likely in a protagonist/antagonist situation, but not unreasonable between two characters who are seeking the same goal.)

   Setting aside any opposition that is crucial to your plot for now, see how many of the complementary adjectives you can replace with nearly synonymous adjectives. For example, if you had *strong* and *weak*, try replacing *weak* with *laid-back, indecisive, indolent, slender,* or even *peace-loving*. No, these are not direct synonyms at all, but that's the point: you're trying to zero in on words that define this character's "weakness" without relying on your primary character's "strength." Does the new list give you a different view of this character?

2. Consider what your story would look like from the secondary character's point of view. If the secondary character were the protagonist, what would he or she want?

3. Try describing a scene from the secondary character's point of view, even in the secondary character's voice. (For an example of this overlapping point of view, take a look at Mary Renault's novels *Fire from Heaven* and *The Mask of Apollo*. The same encounter, between an actor and the young Alexander the Great, is described in both, but from the very different perspectives of the actor—a first-person narrative—and Alexander himself, in *Fire from Heaven*'s omniscient third person. In a large sense, the scene means the same thing, as Renault had an overarching vision of Alexander's history that informed all her historical novels, but to the characters it has very differing meanings.

7

CHAPTER

Research

IT SHOULD BE PRETTY OBVIOUS BY NOW THAT, DESPITE THE fantastic and speculative elements of the genre, science fiction is built on a core of reality. Its "what ifs" take off from agreed fact (or falsehood), and without that base most readers would deny that a story is "really" science fiction. It follows, therefore, that you have to keep up with what's going on in the real world in order to come up with ideas that you can parlay into the kinds of "what ifs" that make complex and interesting novels. Chapter 2 was about that process; this chapter is about some of the tools and techniques you can use to follow up on your original "what if" (although some ideas here may also stimulate new "what ifs").

First, as mentioned previously, you need to be aware of what's happening in the world around you. In a general sense, this means making sure you keep abreast of current events—and not just on television news but in print media as well. In a specifically scientific context, this means keeping track of developing ideas and theories. Given the amount of information available, and the work constantly being done in nearly every field, it's hard, if not impossible, to keep informed about all the sciences. It's often easier to concentrate on several fields that interest you, but that risks missing the odd development in another area that turns out to hold the key to your next story. That's why I would strongly recommend becoming a regular reader of one (or more) of the more general scientific journals. The classic is, of course, *Scientific American*, but there are many others, from *Discover* and *Omni* to *Science*, all of which strive to cover science in general rather than any particular discipline. If you can afford to subscribe to one (or more), I would recommend doing so: you can tear out pages for later reference, file them with your other notes for an idea, and write in the margins, highlight relevant passages, and so on. Also, you get color illustrations without having to go to the expense of color photocopying. If you can't afford to subscribe, the odds are that your local public library will have at least *Scientific American* and probably others as well, and you can read them there. Obviously, you can't write in (or tear pages out of) library copies, but you can easily make photocopies of interesting articles or, cheapest of all, take notes from them. (This is one of the really good reasons to learn to take good notes in school.) I've found that taking written notes does force me to think about what's really important in an article; on the down side, in the early stages of a project, I often overlook something that turns out to be important to the later development of an idea, and have to go back to the article a second time. The moral is to always note your sources well so that you can find them again!

In general, your local public library is a gold mine of information, and you should use it. Once you've found something that interests you, that might make a good "what if," the library is the obvious and best place to start looking into it. Get to know what's available: what magazines and journals the library subscribes to, what on-line resources it offers, what's available in its research section (and what kinds of help the research librarians can offer you), and what the interlibrary loan policies are. Depending on how new or how esoteric the subject is (and on budget constraints and the head librarian's buying decisions), your local library may well have all the information you need to begin working on an idea.

Obviously, start with the card catalog, or, if you're really stumped, ask a librarian for help in setting your search parameters. I think you'll be surprised at how much you're likely to turn up just on first glance. If, however, you don't find anything useful, or, as is more likely, your first research points you to more esoteric subjects, once again the library should be able to help you. It may have reciprocal privileges at a local state university (my local university allows anyone to use their open stacks; if you have a local public library card, you can, for a small fee, check books out as well), or at a library in a larger town where you may find what you need. Even if it doesn't have reciprocal borrower's privileges, it will almost certainly be able to get books by interlibrary loan. This can be a little difficult—most of the time, you need to know the names and authors of the books you're requesting—but you can frequently find that information in the source that originally sparked your interest. (That's one reason to read the footnotes and endnotes.) If not, the librarians can usually help you. They have access to on-line catalogs from other institutions, and to central clearinghouses that usually can turn up what you need. In some libraries, those catalogs are on-line and accessible to the public, and I'd encourage you to use them if they are. This not only places less demand on the librarians (who are usually overworked and underpaid), but also leaves more openings for the kind of serendipity in which the perfect book turns up at the top of the list.

Most of all, never underestimate the ability of a good librarian. When I was working on *Shadow Man*, I wanted to read Hugh Young's *Genital Abnormalities and Hermaphroditism*, which when it was published in 1937 was the standard work on intersexuality. However, since then, a whole new series of studies, surgical techniques, and model of human reproduction have rendered it obsolete except for the handful of case studies. I asked my local library to see if they could find a copy through interlibrary loan, and in fact they were able to locate one in North Carolina and borrow it for me. If you're really stumped with something, ask for help: you never know what a librarian may be able to find for you.

I discussed the idea of cultivating serendipity in Chapter 2, but I've found it to be such an important part of the research process that I want to explore it further here. "Cultivating serendipity" may seem to be a contradiction—how can you plan to look for something that by definition must be found by accident?—but it's the best way I've found to describe an otherwise nebulous process. In essence, there are two ways to approach research. One is to get the name of a reference you want, go to the library (or the Web, or an informed person, or whatever source seems most appropriate) and collect the one answer, then take it home, analyze it, collect another reference, and repeat the process until you've found out everything you wanted to know. The other, and the one that I prefer, is to get the name of a reference, then go to the library (or whatever) and look around the edges of the answer. If you found one book in the card catalog that looks perfect, by all means, read it—but look at the other books on the shelves around it. Is there something else there that would add an interesting dimension to your search? If you're searching the Web, follow a bunch of links; if you're interviewing a person, have more than one question to ask—and be alert to cues about their interests in the subject, even if it's off your track. The thing that they're interested in may be more useful than the idea you started with. Leave yourself room to be surprised, and make sure you look away from your planned path every now and then. The more you do, the more you'll find.

It's also important to remember to listen to the people around you. This applies most obviously when you're dealing with experts in a field, people who've agreed to help you, but it also applies when you're talking to friends and acquaintances, or your fellow writers and fans, about your interests and theirs. You need to stay aware of the nuances of the conversation, and be willing to give up some of your preconceived notions of what is and isn't relevant in order to follow up on their interests. Their perception of cutting-edge ideas, or of what's really important in the field, may take you in new and useful directions, and it's important to leave yourself open to those changes. You may decide not to pursue their thoughts in this story, but you can always file them away for later—and, if nothing else, at least you know that this other facet of the subject exists.

In general, when you approach others for help in a subject, you're asking them to tell you about something that already fascinates them, and this is usually flattering and enjoyable. However, when you're dealing with experts who are also professionals in their field, you owe them a certain level of courtesy: this is their business, after all, and you need to be sensitive to everything that entails. First, if you've encountered them in a social situation, be aware that they, too, are there for fun rather than work, and that there are probably other people around who would like to talk to them (and you).

Experts may not feel like talking about their job in any detail under those circumstances, or may feel that it's inappropriate to go into too much detail in a public setting. Also, you may not know the right questions to ask just at that moment—I've had this happen to me more than once, particularly when I was at the beginning of a project. In general, I've found it best to explain that I'm working on a project that involves their field and to ask them if I may contact them later with a few specific questions, either by e-mail or letter (my preferred method, since it gives the other person control over how and when to respond), or by phone. (I also try to make my request contingent on their having time to talk to me, because that gives them an easy and inoffensive way to say no: "Oh, I'm just snowed under with work right now.") Then I do my research, narrow my questions to things I can't answer from other sources, and follow up on the contact. This should go without saying, but be polite, be concise, and thank people for their time and effort—on the acknowledgments page is always appropriate, though I usually also ask if they mind being listed. The same considerations apply if you're contacting a stranger who is an expert. I generally find it easier to work from a friend's introduction, but that's not always necessary. Be polite, offer people an easy way out of helping you, do your research and have your questions ready, and always abide by any restrictions they set. If, for example, someone says, "sure, give me a call, but not in the mornings," make sure you don't call until after noon.

Acknowledged experts in their profession are only one human resource, however. Particularly in SF, where both writers and readers tend to have professional credentials (often in multiple fields) as well as interests and extensive knowledge in fields that aren't their profession, you often run into what I think of as the expert amateur. These are people who know an awful lot about something just for the pleasure of it—members of the Society for Creative Anachronism, who tend to know very narrow historical subjects in great depth and detail; or amateur musicians who can tell you everything you ever wanted to know about their chosen style; or fellow writers who've just written a book based on some new discovery in biology. These people can be as much help as any professional, and sometimes more so, because this is their avocation, and they enjoy sharing both their knowledge and pleasure in it. However, you do need to be aware that not all of the expert ama- teurs are really experts. A few (though they really are in the minori- ty) simply don't know as much as they pretend, or have built their research on the work of marginal members of the field or on other amateur experts. A larger group are simply unaware of, or unable to keep up with, the most recent developments in their field. Your best bet, in talking to the expert amateurs, is to ask them for further sources as well as information—for the names of journals they read, of good books and scholars to search for, for other experts, amateur and professional, to contact. (This is another place where the research skills you were taught in school will come in handy: you need to check copyright dates, authors' credentials, and their stand- ing in the field.) You should do the same thing with professionals, too, of course, but in that case, because they have to keep up with the current state of their field, you can be somewhat less concerned with double-checking what they have to say. The great thing about asking expert amateurs for help is that they generally combine the soul of a research librarian with the enthusiasm of a teenager: you are likely to get ten times as much information as you expected, and as much help as you can accept.

One final thing to consider, in talking to people, is that the emo- tion behind the facts may be as important a piece of information as the facts themselves. I have heard a story that William Gibson start- ed the work that became the groundbreaking cyberpunk novel *Neuromancer* because he heard computer programmers talking about a "computer virus." This was before the term was in common use, and the metaphor hit him hard: something "inside" the computer that attacked it in the same way that a virus attacks the human body. (Try to imagine that you've never heard the phrase before, and think about the ramifications of it: it says a lot not only about the way we see computers, but also about the existence of the computer world that Gibson named cyberspace.) The programmers were talking about this virus with the same mix of annoyance and disgust that most of us talk about catching a bad cold, and the combination of emotion, fact, and metaphor was the spark from which he ultimately created cyberpunk. The fact that his vision of the Net relied on technologies that were decades if not centuries from development (an understanding of the human nervous system sufficient to allow an implanted direct mind/computer interface) was irrelevant to his grasp of the excitement and emotions that the Net evoked in its first users.

These days, the Net is a daily reality for a lot more of us. The Web in particular is being touted as a wonderful source of information, and is becoming one of the first places people turn when they need to know something. (This was brought home to me when my partner received a note from a friend saying that the friend had been diagnosed with cancer and was scheduled for surgery—on the day before my partner received the letter. The friend lives in a medium-sized town in Iowa; my partner proceeded to the computer, logged onto the Web, and located the only hospital in town. She was able to contact her friend, find out that the surgery was successful, and arrange to send flowers. It was a lot easier and faster than using the telephone.)

The trouble with the Web is also its greatest strength: there is no "governing body" that determines what can and can't be put out there for the world to view. Anyone (or at least anyone who can get access to a computer, a phone line, an ISP or on-line service, and has the time and inclination to master some form of HTML) can put up a Web page on any topic he or she wants to address. A search on that topic (or sometimes on something close to that topic) will then pull up that page—and a good chunk of everything else that's out there (but not necessarily all of it, which is another issue). To give an example, a search on "comet Hale-Bopp" pulled up NASA pages, Jet Propulsion Laboratory pages, a couple of pages by amateur astronomers, and a page telling you where and when to look for the comet. It also pulled up a series of pages claiming variously that Hale-Bopp was the precursor to an alien invasion or some other millennial catastrophe, that it was being shadowed by a "Saturn-like object" identified by one correspondent (from personal experience as an abductee) as a Venusian spacecraft, and that the government, NASA, and/or JPL all knew that this disaster was on the way but were hiding it from the public because there was nothing they could do about it. (This page had links to various survivalist sites that purported to tell you what you should be doing to prepare for whatever it was that was going to happen.) I also found a page that was created to rebut the claims for the Saturn-like object. However, this particular search did not turn up any pages about or created by the Heaven's Gate cult, whose beliefs about the comet led to their mass suicide some months after I consulted the search engines. This is particularly ironic (and sad) considering the Heaven's Gate members were themselves designers of Web pages and had created a large site specifically to inform the world of their beliefs about the comet. It's also an object lesson in the need for care in dealing with the Web: You can never be sure of what you're missing. The Web is ultimately no different from any other research tool: you need to know what you're looking for, and you need to know how to evaluate your sources.

On the Web, the latter becomes slightly more difficult than in more familiar formats. You have not only privately maintained pages, whose owners may be professionals, expert amateurs, or ignorant enthusiasts, but also professionally maintained pages that are put up by companies with products to sell and organizations with points of view to promote. In part, the problem stems from two different models of the Web that coexist, occasionally even on the same page. First there is the Web as information provider: a source for (to name a few) scholarly papers, conference notes, newspaper and wire service stories, and individual scholars. Then there is the Web as communications service, in which people are given ways to connect to other people, goods, and services. There are virtual reality (VR) chat rooms, band pages that list tour schedules and personal information, book review journals, and, of course, the whole "virtual mall" phenomenon. A heart disease page that is maintained by a drug company with a stake in a particular treatment obviously conforms to both models. When you use the Web as a resource, you have to make sure you know which model your sources are using, and how they fit into the larger context surrounding the issue you're researching. For example, when I'm looking into Web publishing, to mention a topic I'm currently tracking, I treat daily newspapers, industry journals, and a fascinating public relations newsletter site differently. They're all accurate, but a daily newspaper often misstates or overemphasizes particular technical details that industry journals get absolutely right. On the other hand, few of the journals spend much time questioning the basic assumptions of the virtual communities, as the daily papers frequently do. And the PR newsletter, while keeping me up-to-date on all the latest developments and releases from the major (and minor) software companies, doesn't tell me much about those companies' failures. You need to read the Web with care and attention, not treat it as a neutral source.

Beyond the Web lies the world of newsgroups and mailing lists. These raise the same questions of source and reliability as Web sites, but offer fewer ways of checking their contributors' accuracy. A lot depends on the attitude and shared interests of the people who post regularly—a newsgroup for people who have or have had cancer has a different tone from a newsgroup dedicated to guitar amplifier repair, and still different from the groups dedicated to fans of written science fiction. People do regularly claim credentials—as doctors, lawyers, tube amp repair technicians, and so on—but it's worth remembering that you have only their word for it when you're reading a newsgroup. There aren't many outright liars out there, but there are a few, and in the heat of argument people are prone to exaggerate their qualifications. Even professionals can give bad advice if they stray outside their particular area of expertise, and professionals of equal skill and status can, and do, disagree as to the best way to handle a problem. To a certain extent the groups are self-correcting, as people post comments, corrections, and "flames" in response to bad information, but you may miss some corrections, and bad information may remain in circulation for a long time.

Mailing lists are subject to the same considerations, though they at least have the advantage of bringing the information directly to your mailbox. In general, though, you should double-check any fact that you find first on the Net, unless you know the source and know that it's reliable on this topic. If you engage in newsgroup or mailing list discussions, and decide to rely on something somebody told you in that context, check either the fact or their credentials, or both—or be sure you don't care if they turn out to be well-known lunatics. Most of the time, people will be who they claim to be, and have all the skills they claim to have; you may even find yourself asking questions of someone who's just finished prize-winning research in the field you're studying. (Or, as happened to me, you may find that someone you know in a totally different context also knows a lot about the subject you're working on. I mentioned my then in-progress novel, *Burning Bright*, which involves a complicated role-playing game, to an on-line friend who turned out also to be not only a gamer and Game Master, but also active in several national gaming organizations.) However, as in the off-line world, there are people who enjoy misleading others, or who are pushing hidden agendas. Because on-line communication lacks some of the cues, verbal and textual, that we're used to using, it's important to be aware of those differences when relying on it.

Facts and extrapolation are vital to a science fiction novel, but they remain dull and static without feeling to give them life. While I'm not advocating that you go out of your way to find experiences that stretch your emotional range, there are some things that you can do to help yourself imagine and convey a variety of feelings. The first, and simplest, is to cultivate a habit of observation, of being aware of what you see, hear, and feel and how you can turn these perceptions into words that will let the reader share your experience. I think many, maybe even most, writers have a corner of their minds always turned to writing, a part of the brain that's always analyzing the world around them for useful ideas and images. Sometimes that work gets done at a subconscious level, but it's helpful to develop an awareness of the process as well. One of the simplest ways to do this is periodically to stop yourself and ask, "How would I write this?" If you're outside on a clear night and the stars are vivid overhead, think about how you would describe them. Do they really twinkle? Is it dark enough for you to see the Milky Way, or is the sky the flat brown-black of an urban night? What does the air feel like, and what are the sounds like? Do voices carry differently in the dark, or is this a place where night and day aren't that distinct any more? If you're hanging out with friends, really listen to the conversation for a little bit. Pay attention to the ways that people run sentences together, use mixed grammar and clichés, and then sometimes say something so perfect that it's like a slap in the face. How many times have you heard the same argument between two people, as well as what's under the surface? Is it teasing, a way of reinforcing an old bond, or is it a symptom of something deeper? How would you show all of that, all the complexities of their relationship, without actually telling your readers all the details of their past history? If you work out regularly, or play a sport, pay attention to the way your body feels when you're exerting yourself. It may all "hurt," but there's a huge difference between the "good" pain that comes from pushing yourself to the limits and the pain of an injury. Is "blue" really a good enough description of the ocean, and are sunsets always "fiery"? The idea is to get beyond the habitual, to begin writing from what you see is really there rather than what you've been told to see.

Of course, this may seem less than useful in science fiction, a field in which you're unlikely to have experienced the majority of the things you're describing. While it's true that you and most of your readers will not have been into space or surfed the Web via a brain implant, most will have been afraid, or ecstatic, or overworked, or whatever adjective best describes your protagonist's state of mind. The more you can convince your readers that you really know what it feels like to do something they do know about, the easier it is for them to believe you when you tell them what it's really like to take an FTL ship through hyperspace.

There are a number of techniques you can call on to help you expand on your own experiences. Observation is probably the first and best: being aware of how you (and your friends, acquaintances, and enemies) react to the world around you. I've been on panels where the process was described as a kind of vampirism, battening on to other people's emotions as well as your own, but I think Esther Friesner described it best on a panel we both attended. She called it *scavenging*, nosing through your own and your friends' emotional roadkill and picking out the usable bits. I think she's right in this: it's not an angst-ridden process, or often even a conscious decision, but something as basic and as necessary as eating. You shouldn't let everybody know what you're doing—your friends won't thank you for splashing their pain across your pages, particularly if they don't come off very well in the process, nor will your family be happy if, at your grandfather's funeral, you announce that you now know how to write a certain scene. But these kinds of experiences are legitimate sources to draw on in your work, and you should not neglect them.

The other way of investigating emotions you've never experienced is through imagination, your own or other people's. Obviously, if you want to be a writer, you should read widely. You not only learn about craft and style, but also are exposed to other people's finely honed, well-presented emotional experiences. You're also more likely to encounter extreme emotions and behaviors in novels, and those are generally a lot more pleasant to experience through fiction than in real life. Another method is the actor's exercise of starting with an emotion that you have experienced, and then expanding on it until you can imagine something you've never really felt. Not many of us have killed people, but most of us have been angry at someone. Many of us have been angry enough to strike another person, or at least to have wanted to. Take that emotion, remember it—the ache in the jaw from clenching the teeth, the way anger literally took your breath away, whatever it is you remember most clearly—and expand it in your mind until it's large enough to make homicide comprehensible. You can use the same basic technique of starting with something that you do know to reach most of the extremes of human experience.

Sometimes you'll find that a character needs to react in a way that you can't imagine yourself behaving, not just to preserve the mechanics of the plot, but because events and everything you've set up about the character lead to this action. This is a place where the distance you developed between yourself and the character is important: you're looking not for what you would feel or do, but for how your character would react. By concentrating on these differences, you may be able to determine what the character has to do, and then draw on things you've seen other people do to help you write that scene. As a last resort, you may have to find a way to write around your own weakness. For example, when I was working on *Burning Bright*, it became clear that one of the point of view characters, an artist named Ransome, had to die at the end of the novel, and had to die because of a stupid mistake, through misjudging the reaction of a long-time enemy. I found the idea of fatal carelessness really unattractive, and therefore really hard to write. It was perfectly in keeping with the character as he'd been presented, but it was hard for me to imagine, especially under the particular circumstances of the scene. Finally, I resolved the problem in two ways. First, I told the death scene from the point of view of another of Ransome's enemies, someone who had never really understood the motivation behind any of Ransome's actions. This let me write the scene without really understanding why Ransome had made this mistake: Damian Chrestil didn't understand it, either. Second, I added a scene immediately before the death that gave Ransome an implied reason to become more careless than usual. The situation stemmed from emotions that I found powerful and could write convincingly. It seems to have worked: I've had lots of people say that they wished Ransome hadn't been killed, but no one has ever complained that they didn't understand why he made the mistake.

Inevitably, another source of ideas and inspiration will be other people's SF novels. As long as it doesn't devolve into outright plagiarism, this is actually a good thing. Science fiction, like most genre writing, depends on convention as well as on original ideas. It is a field with a rich history and an established culture, and there is no other way to learn both the conventions and the culture than by reading widely. If you can't find science fiction that you like to read, given the breadth and depth of the field today, you may be working in the wrong genre.

Contemporary science fiction builds heavily on the works of its acknowledged masters. In this basic concept, it's not that different from any other kind of fiction (including mainstream); however, the way that this works out in practice means that writers are not only building stylistically on each other's work but also responding to each other's ideas and the devices that embody them. A truly revolutionary idea, like Gibson's conception of cyberspace, rapidly becomes a new convention as other writers accept or reject Gibson's vision of the world built from the personal computer. (For those of you who've grown up with the desktop machine, it might be instructive to go back and read some of the novels based on the previous model of computer/human interaction: anything from Clarke and Kubrik's 2001 to Gerrold's *When Harlie Was One* to Heinlein's *The Moon Is a Harsh Mistress* to the ship's computers of Poul Anderson's *The Trouble Twisters* and *Star Trek*. Note that *Star Trek* has never caught up with the computer revolution. The monolithic and inaccessible mainframe, which functions as an inscrutable but physically present and frequently overbearing Other, is a completely different vision from the idea of multiple computers creating space and function.) The only way to become part of this conversation is to read other people's work: science fiction is a complex and sophisticated field, and you can't just walk in cold and expect to come up with a concept that knocks people's socks off. Not only that, but the majority of science fiction readers are at least as knowledgeable as the writers, and often more so. Many of them have read almost everything that has been published since they turned fourteen, and they are deeply aware of how any author's work fits into that larger context. They won't be shy about telling you if you've used a familiar idea in a familiar way. Probably the most common failing for newer writers, particularly those coming into the field from other forms of literature, is to assume that, because SF is a genre and reliant on convention, they don't need to have more than a superficial acquaintance with the field. This results in ideas that everyone who knows the field has already seen many times, but that seem new and fresh to the writer. The classic example of this, which is not, I regret to say, apocryphal, is the story of a spaceship that crashes on an uninhabited planet, killing all but two of the crew, who after much struggle manage to survive—and who are named, as revealed in the final paragraph, Adam and Eve. This one is common enough to be explicitly banned in a couple of magazines' submissions information. (This is not to say that a story on this theme *couldn't* sell, but it would have to be done with a new twist and the awareness that it is rehashing something trite before an editor would even look at it.)

The other reason to read other people's writing is to study your own craft. When you read science fiction, you should always be aware of what you like and dislike about a book, and why you feel that way. What makes your favorite novels so memorable, and how do the authors produce those effects? Is it just the idea, or is it a combination of idea, character, and writing that grabs your attention? What do your favorite authors do to make their characters attractive to you, or to make their settings realistic? What do they do that you want to be able to do—and what do they do that you wish they'd stop? What makes a book a good junk read as opposed to something too stupid to finish—is it characters, plot, idea, setting, or something else that lets you enjoy the novel on its own terms? In other words, while I hope you never stop reading for the sheer pleasure of discovering a new story, it's important to read with attention as well. The more you understand about how other people achieve their effects and create their style, the more control you'll have of your own voice.

The question of reading other people's writing always raises the twin fears of lack of originality and, at the extreme, outright plagiarism. Many new writers seem to feel that if they read other people's work they will inevitably produce inferior copies of that work rather than finding their own voices. Worse still, they fear they will inadvertently copy something from a novel they barely remember reading, and will be branded as plagiarists forever. While plagiarism does occasionally occur, even by mistake as in these writers' nightmares, it is not as common as they fear. It's hard to copy enough of someone else's work to count as plagiarism without doing it on purpose. (And I guess I should say it explicitly: copying other people's work, or even playing in other people's universes without their express permission, crosses the line. You can't do it for profit—that definitely becomes illegal—and it's questionable whether you should do it in private. There's a long tradition of fans writing stories based on the work, and in the worlds, of their favorite writers and television shows, occasionally with the consent and invitation of the artists involved, and it's been said that this helps inexperienced writers learn how to construct a story. While the support that fan writers get from their fellows may be useful, the one thing fan fiction doesn't—can't—teach you is how to create a story that commands attention on its own merit, without the appeal of the original source to draw your reader in. And without that, your own writing can't go anywhere.)

The question of originality is a more subtle one. On the one hand, new ideas, new ways of seeing the world and recreating it as fiction, are always desirable; on the other, science fiction is legitimately a field full of conventions and conventional ways of handling certain themes. Rather than allowing yourself to be paralyzed by the fear that someone, somewhere, might have had your idea before, I'd suggest aiming for a middle ground. In the first place, science fiction is a community as well as a genre: SF writers know each other and talk to each other, and it's not uncommon for a writer to e-mail four or five friends with an interesting tidbit she's discovered. A writer might also send a photocopy of an article to someone he knows is interested in a particular topic. When you combine this habit of sharing interests with a shared and limited set of science sources (after all, how many major discoveries are there likely to be in any field in a year?), you get what I think of as the hive-mind phenomenon. All of a sudden a cluster of writers will publish books dealing with the same broad topic—nanotechnology, perhaps, or voudoun—or there will be a sudden upsurge in a neglected corner of the genre, such as space opera. The books are usually very different, and the timing of publication makes it clear that everybody was simply working on the same broad idea at the same time. (This happened to me with my Silence Leigh trilogy. Brian Daley published a trilogy, *Tales of the White Ship Avatar*, featuring a character called Alacrity Fitzhugh, which, like my trilogy, was unabashed space opera with a fairly fantastic underlying premise. The books are otherwise completely different, and I enjoyed his enormously—Daley was particularly brilliant at inventing new technical jargon, as well as a great storyteller—but it was disconcerting to realize that a complete stranger had not only written the same style of book, but chosen the same kind of name for one of his protagonists.)

There's nothing either good or bad about this. Most of the time, the writers involved will have chosen sufficiently different approaches to the subject to leave room for all of them to find an audience. The trickier situation arises when someone uses an idea for the first time, and other writers read that novel and discover that they want to explore other aspects of the same theme, or simply handle it differently. However, this is perfectly legitimate. A new novel then becomes another entry into the dialogue on this particular theme. For example, Brin's *Glory Season* is his response to the many books dealing with feminism and biology; his debt to his predecessors is more explicitly acknowledged than most, in that he names many of his fictional towns after important feminist writers of the 1970s and 1980s. In general, shared experience produces similar fiction: SF writers are largely looking at the same real-world issues, and are likely to cope by writing about them. There is nothing wrong with joining the conversation.

Whether you're approaching a familiar idea in a new way or working with a "what if" that no one's ever seen before, you need to be able to convince your readers that your extrapolation is the best and most logical progression—that it's the way things are going to be. Even if their belief lasts only for the length of the book, it has to be there for them to make the effort to finish the story. The only way you can earn that belief is by doing the research, and enough research that you can convince professionals in the field that you share their knowledge. This can be hard work, particularly if it's a field that you don't know well, but the payoff is highly worthwhile.

8

CHAPTER

Putting It All Together

AT SOME POINT IN YOUR WRITING, YOU'RE GOING TO HAVE TO stop doing research, or writing character sketches and plot exercises, and start putting all the pieces together into a single whole. Your "what if" has to lead logically into the plot, inform the setting and the characters, and all of that has to be solidly grounded in the research you've done. And somehow, you also have to tell an exciting story that feels in some way different from anything else your readers have encountered. Put that way, writing sounds like an arduous, even impossible, task, but there are a number of things you can do to make it easier, and to keep the fun alive. After all, if writing isn't more fun than not, there's no point in doing it: you can make a far better living (and achieve a higher social and intellectual status) doing almost anything else instead of writing science fiction.

Before you start working seriously on a manuscript, you should have worked out a "what if," done your research on the science involved, and have your main characters and their setting well in mind. You should probably also have an idea of the story you want to tell, and know what kind of story it is as well as what you want to make happen in it. After all, the kind of story—serious consideration of scary problems or lighthearted adventure; hard-core technical SF or wildly speculative science fantasy—influences both the structure and the style you'll want to use. Now it's time to start working out the details of the plot. Some people start by making an outline, using broad event headers and going back to fill in the lesser details after the more important things are in place. The great advantage to this format is that it makes you see the overall shape of the plot—the exposition, climaxes, and denouement—and helps you to keep it in mind from the beginning. Other people sit down and write an informal proposal, a not-for-public-consumption version of the proposals experienced novelists use to sell their books. Proposals are difficult to write well, particularly as a sales tool, and it's almost impossible to sell a novel on a proposal alone unless you have a proven track record, but they can be handy at this stage. In essence, a proposal is a synopsis of the story you want to tell. It's a condensed version, but all the important elements of events and motivation should be there, or you should know that they are missing and already be planning to add them. Try writing the proposal as if you were going to show it to an agent or publisher; this will help you remember to include things that you might otherwise leave out. What I find useful about doing this kind of proposal is that, in creating the flow of the story, I tend to see new possibilities, particularly connections between events, that I hadn't seen before.

For other people, however, working out a plot in that kind of detail kills their desire to write the actual novel. (This is the same reason that many experienced writers and writing books tell you not to spend too much time talking about your ideas. It wastes time you could spend writing, and, more important, after you've worked out the plot in excruciating detail, you may no longer want to write it.) For people who feel this way, it's enough to know a few high points—landmarks that they're aiming for—like the major climax and the ending; the rest they invent or discover as they go along. The major disadvantage to plunging straight into the story is that you're more likely to have to rewrite sections—or do entire fresh drafts—as you discover new things you want to say. However, the people I know who work this way don't regard this as extra work, but as a vitally important part of their creative process.

None of these methods has any inherent superiority. What works for you may not work for your best friend or for anybody else in your writing group, and it may not work for you on your next project. The important thing is to be aware of the possibilities, and to try several different methods until you've found a reliable way to begin working. I've tried most of them, and have settled on a modified proposal method, in which I summarize the events of the first third of the novel in detail, and sketch out the middle and end in more general terms. Lately, however, I've found myself finishing the first third of a manuscript and realizing that I need to refocus the entire project—which involved rewriting the sections already completed—so I'm going to use a different approach with my next novel. I'll probably try outlining first, because the problem seems to be not seeing the overall story as clearly as I should. It's always useful, if you find yourself having problems, to take a look at what you're doing, and see if some other method might work better for you. Even if it's just a temporary change, the break may free up your subconscious and let you find a new way to resolve the problem.

Once you have an idea of the plot, of the story you want to tell, you can start at the beginning, or jump in at some exciting point in your outline. However, no matter where you start, you find yourself having to make decisions about point of view, voice, and general narrative style. Sometimes, those choices have already been made at a subconscious level, so that you find that there really is only one way that you want to tell this story—a first-person narrative, maybe, or a complex third-person with multiple points of view. More often, though, you can see several possibilities, each with strengths and weaknesses, and it's hard to know which one to choose. The best way I've found to resolve the question is to find a way to try each of the options. Choose a situation—a full scene or an incident; even a description or a conversation between two characters can give you enough material to start with—and write it using the voice that seems to come most naturally to it. Let yourself play with the scene; it's not going to be part of the final draft, and you don't even have to finish it. Use this chance to try out ideas and voices you wouldn't normally try, or that you don't think would work over the long run. Then choose another situation, and do it again. Try a different voice this time, or a different point of view character; try switching from first to third person, or vice versa. As you work on these sketches, you'll probably find that the perfect voice, point of view, and style become clear to you.

It's also possible to approach the same problem more analytically, and that can also be useful if none of the sketches seems to be developing into quite what you were looking for. Each of the various components—the setting, characters, "what if," plot, structure, and voice—should reinforce each other, and add up to the best presentation of your story. Here's another place where it can be extremely useful to take a look at where you fit into the genre. I'm not advocating imitation of whatever is hot right now; what I am suggesting is that you might be able to learn something, or at least get a new perspective on your particular problem, by looking at how other novels with similar tone have been constructed. Since you've chosen to work within a genre, you should use it to your advantage.

The most important factor in this is probably reader expectation. This hearkens back to the idea of the contract between writer and reader introduced in Chapter 1. By presenting your story as science fiction, you set up certain basic expectations—that the story will be set in a place, and probably a time, somehow significantly different from the present, and that it will nonetheless reflect things about contemporary society. Your choices of voice and style also set up expectations, though these are somewhat more subtly defined. A reader expects that the voice you choose will work with the story, not against it, and that any major changes in voice will be fairly presented. In other words, if you intend for your novel to start out as a light comedy, but to end as heavy melodrama, there needs to be a reason for it, and you need to take your readers with you as the characters' situation changes, not simply declare in the last three chapters that tragedy has struck and all these people must now make the best of it. If your story needs to include the perspectives of many different characters, you'll probably want to choose a form of third-person narrative, and you need to signal to your readers as early as possible that the points of view will change, so that they will expect and be prepared for them. If you're going to choose an apparently humorous voice or potentially silly situation, you need to make sure readers can tell that you intend to be funny, or that you're actually being very serious under the ironic glaze of the narrative voice. (Jonathan Lethem's *Gun, with Occasional Music* is a good example of a novel that does this.) A story that wavers between two forms without some clues to the author's intentions tends to make readers uncomfortable rather than curious.

Within the genre itself, there are a number of subgenres and sty-
listic conventions that you can use to your advantage as well. Most
of these are grounded in solid technique, which is one of the reasons they've become conventions. For example, the massive,
sprawling novels based around a single hard-science "what if"—
such as Kim Stanley Robinson's *Mars* trilogy or Frank Herbert's
Dune—tend to be written in a rather distant third person, and to feature a large cast of point of view characters. There are good reasons
for this. For one thing, the subject is usually complex in its details,
and, while it's interesting in its own right, it becomes more interesting to readers if they have more than one view of it to consider.
It's also easier to expand on those details if there is a large cast of
characters, all of whom have good reason to be interested in different aspects of the central idea. The large cast, and its complex interactions, also provides a wider range of plot possibilities than a single "what if" usually can. After all, the promise of a novel is that it
will be about people (in the broadest possible sense—beings with
whom readers can identify, whom they can care about) rather than
things, and readers of novels have a right to see that expectation
fulfilled. The *Mars* novels are not just about the settlement of Mars,
but about the people who settle the planet, and their personal and
political relationships. (*Moby Dick* is not a novel about a whale; it's
a novel about people hunting for a particular whale.) More experimental ideas may have more experimental forms—that's one of the
ways a writer can signal that a story will not follow the familiar conventions—or they may have a simpler structure, so that the experimental parts of the idea can have full play. Joanna Russ's *The Female
Man* uses a nonlinear structure to point out the revolutionary nature
of her "what ifs"; its very strangeness allows nervous readers to distance themselves from the weird and upsetting worlds. On the other
hand, Suzy McKee Charnas's trilogy, *Walk to the End of the World*,
Motherlines, and *The Furies*, is couched in relatively straightforward
narrative that allows readers to find their way more easily in these
extremely unfamiliar, and intentionally disturbing, settings.

One way of looking at this process is to stay aware of your
"strangeness budget" (see Chapter 3). Its size can vary from story to
story. On the one hand, readers picking up a novel about exploring

an alien world or making contact with an alien civilization expect a fairly large number of strange and unfamiliar things, and are willing to tolerate a high level of uncertainty because it fits the story. On the other, readers picking up a near-future thriller (these generally assume that not much has changed between now and then) are not likely to be comfortable with being expected to learn terms in four unfamiliar languages while imagining both a new aeronautical jargon and a whole new model for the Internet. I've seen some perfectly decent stories destroyed by the authors' decision to use an invented term for every single thing, from clothing to tableware to the fittings of the spaceship. In general, it's safer to be sparing with invented terms, and to save the strangeness budget for more important things, like the concepts behind your "what if."

Of course, you do have to provide enough background for your invented words, worlds, and people to make sense to your readers, and that brings up the dreaded task of exposition. Too often, you can look at a manuscript and see the point at which the writer realized he or she had to explain a large chunk of background—and did exactly that, with several long paragraphs of description or a speech beginning, "As you know . . ." (This is usually described as an expository lump or an info dump.) The big chunks of description tend to stop the narrative dead while the writer makes the needed explanation; if the readers don't skim or skip it outright (and so miss important information), you have to win their attention all over again when the description is finished. The trouble with "as you know . . ." speeches is exactly that: if the characters really do know it, why don't the people being addressed break in and say so? They would in the real world. How do you strike a balance between the constraints of the strangeness budget and your very real need to let your readers know the information they need to make sense of the story? There are a number of methods. Most novels end up using some combination of different techniques, but the object remains the same: to get the exposition in without overspending the budget.

One of the classic techniques is the "galactic encyclopedia entry." This is exactly what it says it is: an invented definition or description or excerpt from an imaginary history text that gives the reader vital information in the style of the culture. These are usually presented as forewords or as chapter headings. People often think of this as a Golden Age method, and in fact Isaac Asimov's Foundation trilogy, often considered the apotheosis of Golden Age writing, begins with a biographical entry from the *Encyclopedia Galactica* describing the person who will become the main character. The advantage to the method is that it puts the important information right up front, in a format that lets readers know that they need to pay attention to it; it also lets you fill in background that could be difficult to present any other way, such as exact dates, or precise definitions of an unfamiliar term, or salient details of the story's setting. If done with a good ear for language and style, the way the entries are written can tell the readers quite a bit about the society that wrote the text, or that considers it a reliable source. (The mere name of the text frequently quoted in the chapter headings of *Dune*—the *Orange Catholic Bible*—helps tell you something about the society's religious beliefs.) However, many readers (and writers) consider this to be a clumsy, old-fashioned technique, more suited to space opera than to serious science fiction, and, if handled badly, it can weigh the story down with lots of meaningless information.

I've used the technique in *Dreamships* and in *Dreaming Metal* to set the physical and political stage quickly. It was vital in *Dreamships* that readers know from the beginning that economic and political power on Persephone, where most of the novel takes place, are held by two different groups and that this division is a source of constant tension. In *Dreaming Metal*, because the entire novel takes place on Persephone among characters who are primarily concerned with the affairs of that world, it was important to make sure that readers knew from the beginning that Persephone was part of a larger multiplanetary society. In each case, I began the book with an entry from an unnamed travel guide purporting to offer the basic information an interstellar traveler would need before visiting Persephone. (With *Dreamships*, to help offset the old-fashioned feeling of the form, I followed it with an epigraph from a song called "Halleluiah Man" that captured much of the feeling that I wanted to convey in the novel.) I also used the same "Standard Planetary Register" format in *The Kindly Ones*, where the custom of "social death" producing living people who were treated as "ghosts" had to be spelled out at the beginning. I've also used glossary entries as chapter headings in *Shadow Man*, where the invented language was pushing the limits of the strangeness budget, and I didn't want to force readers to turn to the included glossary to find the most important definitions. A more sophisticated version of this technique is the invented news headline or advertising fragment embedded in the story either as a chapter heading or within the text itself. Because they tend to be smaller, these are more useful in providing atmosphere than in giving vital information, but handled right these devices can be richly evocative. Walter Jon Williams uses snatches of advertising banners to great advantage in *Metropolitan*, where the words and images float against the city skies in ironic contrast to the protagonist's pinched, impoverished life.

Another classic means of providing exposition is to structure your story so that the protagonist and the reader learn the necessary information at the same time. In the classic form, the protagonist is a stranger to the place or situation and his or her primary goal in the story is to figure out what's going on. Both Robert A. Heinlein's *Citizen of the Galaxy* and M. J. Engh's *Rainbow Man* share this underlying structure, though the novels are otherwise very different. In the Heinlein tale, the protagonist, a young man named Thorby, begins the novel literally as a *tabula rasa*: he is sold as a child to an old beggar who turns out to be something quite different. As Thorby grows up under the beggar's tutelage, he learns the ways of his world, and the reader learns with him. When the beggar is killed, Thorby escapes into the new and wildly different society of Free Traders, and the reader learns its rules and traditions as Thorby does. When Thorby's fortunes change a final time, once again the reader learns with Thorby. In *Rainbow Man*, the protagonist decides to leave the FTL ship on which she has lived for many years and settle on the planet Bimran. This is a spur-of-the-moment decision, and can't be anything else, due to the limits of the society's technology. Even the fact that she is considered male under local law—she has been sterilized, and the legal definition of a man is a human being incapable of bearing children—does not change her mind. As she learns the rules and the complexities of the local society, the reader learns with her, and the story unwinds at the pace at which she learns.

A variation on this is to place your protagonists in a situation that is unfamiliar to them, and have the unraveling of the situation form the bulk of the plot. Hal Clement's classic *Mission of Gravity* is an excellent example of this method. *Mission of Gravity* is set on an extremely heavy-gravity world that human beings are attempting to study and that also hosts an intelligent native population. The novel is told from the point of view of a native trading-ship captain, Barlennan, who at the beginning of the story has encountered a human spaceship that has landed near the planet's equator, the only place on the world where the gravity is low enough for human beings to tolerate. The orbiting research ship has lost one of its study rockets, which has crashed near the planetary pole, where the gravity is too high for humans to have any hope of recovery, and the researchers persuade Barlennan and his crew to recover the rocket for them. Over the course of the novel, Barlennan has to cross land and seas that he does not know, and, more importantly, to cross from normal to very light gravity (by his standards, anyway) and back to normal again. Barlennan knows his world and the process of sailing its seas as well as anyone does, but he is crossing unfamiliar territory; between his explorations and the human researchers' attempts at help and need for explanation, the reader comes to understand the peculiar physics of this high-gravity world.

Arthur C. Clarke's *Rendezvous with Rama* uses a similar structure. The crew members of the Endeavour, the Solar Survey ship assigned to investigate the object christened Rama, know their collective job and their individual responsibilities extremely well. However, as the different officers and crew interact with each other, explaining their theories and ideas, the reader is in effect told what each person does and how the technology involved works. At the same time, Rama itself is explained only insofar as the crew is able to deduce its functions from physical evidence. The plot of *Dune* relies in part on the readers' learning false stories along with Paul, and learning with him that they are false. Asimov's *The Naked Sun* uses the structure of a mystery, which must for various plot reasons be investigated by a foreign police officer. In this case, the situation—the murder and the mechanics of an investigation—are completely familiar to the protagonist; however, the facts and the setting are as strange to him as they are to the reader. My own *Shadow Man* has two main characters, one of whom is an off-worlder unfamiliar with planetary society even after several years of working on that planet. Their interactions convey most of the information I need to tell my readers.

This way of handling exposition works very well when you want to tell a story from the outside—when you want your protagonist to begin in an unfamiliar situation and gradually learn how it works. In fact, in novels like *Citizen of the Galaxy*, Maureen McHugh's *China Mountain Zhang*, and *Rainbow Man*, this expository method produces a form of picaresque novel, in which a largely rootless protagonist journeys toward an understanding both of the situation and of himself or herself. As discussed in the Introduction, SF offers a chance to make certain abstract ideas concrete and literal; in this case, SF makes the picaresque hero's inner journey as real as his outer journeying. In purely practical terms, a protagonist who doesn't know the situation is more likely to notice and comment on the things you need your readers to know, or to have things explained to her that your readers also need explained to them.

However, if you want to tell a story from inside the situation—a story about someone who is familiar with and part of the novel's setting—this technique is much less effective. The problem here is to figure out how plausibly to tell your readers things that your characters already know. In some cases, all you need to do is to give your characters reasons to notice and comment on important bits of information. A starship pilot could quite believably compare and contrast two different versions of an FTL drive, and in the process provide your readers with a thumbnail sketch of how the basic system works. Another way to handle the problem is to give one of your characters a compelling reason to tell another the information that your readers need to know. This allows you to break up what would otherwise be a solid chunk of data into a natural conversational pattern (question and response, discussion and comment), but you have to take care to make the conversation necessary, and therefore believable.

In working with this kind of expository dialogue, I find it very helpful to keep in mind a concept I first encountered in playwright Jeffrey Sweet's excellent *The Dramatist's Toolkit*. (Because dialogue was difficult for me when I was starting out, I read a lot of books on play-writing to find new techniques and hone my skills.) Sweet intro-duced the idea of low-context versus high-context dialogue. Low-context dialogue occurs between people who don't share a common context, a common understanding of the matter under discussion. Most teaching situations are low-context; so are most doctor/patient relationships or relationships between skilled craftspeople and their customers. High-context dialogue occurs between people who do have that common context, a shared understanding of the matter under discussion. This would cover dialogue between peers working on a professional problem, between people who share a common hobby, or between long-term partners. (The ultimate example of high-context conversation is the kind of shorthand con-versations you hear among people who have been living together for a long time: "Honey—?" "Hall table." "Thanks." It makes no sense to strangers, and friends giggle, but this is a conversation worn down to the essential knowledge that one person forgets medica-tion she is supposed to carry at all times.) The same two people can have either high- or low-context conversations depending on the subject under discussion. For example, if I ask my friend Philip for help changing my car's headlight, the ensuing conversation will be low-context; I don't know much about cars, and I don't know how to change the headlight. On the other hand, when our conversation strays to mutual acquaintances, it becomes high-context. Neither one of us has to tell the other who the people are, or why it's impor-tant that a certain person no longer goes to a certain club.

So one obvious way to create expository dialogue is to make sure that your characters have a low-context conversation about the information your readers need to know. The difficulty, of course, is making sure that these characters would in fact have a low-con-text conversation on that particular topic. For example, two police-men would be unlikely to have a low-context discussion of proper investigative procedure. ("All right, Bob. Our next step will be to take fingerprints." "Oh, I see, Joe.") On the other hand, two law enforcement workers from different branches of their service—a forensic scientist who normally does not do fieldwork, and a homi-cide detective—could more reasonably have a variation of that conversation. Sometimes you can use the tension between shared contexts and special knowledge as a way to place exposition. In my own *Night Sky Mine*, it was important that readers understand the differences among three major social groups, and the prejudices held by each of them about the others. By telling the scene from the point of view of a character who was a member of one group, the Union, but who worked for the Citizen government, and whose job it was to translate between the two groups, I was able to balance explicit exposition with indirect explanations as Rangsey made his decisions about what he would translate, and how.

The low-context/high-context division can be a useful tool outside of dialogue, as well. For example, the old stand-by scene in which the protagonist regards him or herself in a mirror so that the writer can describe the character rarely works when it's that baldly stated. People look at themselves in the mirror every day, usually without commenting on their own high cheekbones or blue eyes or cleft chin. That should be a high-context moment, and therefore exposition or detailed description jars. On the other hand, if you give a character a reason to look at him or herself—an actor putting on makeup, or a businessperson concerned to look his best for an important meeting, or a murderer concerned to hide a new scar from an old friend—then it's possible to slip in a little description without it seeming false. The same holds true for description of setting or society: it's a good idea to give your characters reasons to notice anything they see constantly. To give a real-world example, how many people who are not car buffs notice the make and model of every car they pass on the street? Most of us would notice a Model-T Ford because it's an antique and unusual; many of us notice conspicuously expensive or uncommon cars, like Bentleys or MGs, though we might not be able to identify the model. I happen to notice old Volkswagens because a friend restores them. Even enthusiasts might notice only those models that particularly interested them. By planning carefully, the same passage can tell your readers not only about your world, but about the character who is looking at it.

However, if you choose a character trait to allow your characters to see and describe something, be sure that it's something that won't inconvenience you later. In my second novel, *Five-Twelfths of*

Heaven, I needed a reason for the protagonist and point of view character, Silence Leigh, to be aware enough of homunculi (the bottle-grown nonliving creatures that substituted, in this universe, for conventional robots) to notice and describe them. However, I'd already established that she was a starship's pilot, and that homunculi were common around spaceports; there was no real reason for her to pay more attention to one of them than she would to a cargo crane. I decided, therefore, that she had a personal aversion to them—their size and lumpy shape and the weird texture of their skin made her uncomfortable—so that she was hyperaware of their presence. Unfortunately, as *Five-Twelfths* and its sequels unfolded, it became clear to me that it would have been much easier for me (and for the characters) if Silence did not dislike homunculi so thoroughly, and I had to do some rather complicated plotting to get around her inability to work with them.

Of course, it's also possible to immerse your characters, and your readers, in your world without explanation, and trust that they will figure it out on their own. This is, obviously, a difficult technique to master. It's easy to tell too much, and include lumps, or, more commonly, to tell too little, to get too deep into your characters' world, and to forget to add cues that let readers make the connections they need to figure out the larger context of what's happening. When done right, immersion is enormously effective, and some writers (like Samuel R. Delany, in *Stars in My Pockets Like Grains of Sand*) have made brilliant use of the uncertainties inherent in the form. (Delany redefines the use of pronouns, so that they refer not to gender but to the relationship between the parties.) Terry Dowling uses this technique in *Rynosseros* and his other collections of short fiction, and in his case can rely on his ear for language to carry his readers with him.

In general, though, most writers use some combination of these techniques to slide necessary exposition into their work. All of them offer advantages as well as disadvantages, and each situation you create will call for a different solution. If you find yourself either with too little explanation, or with an expository lump, it's often helpful to sit back and take a look at the context of the scene. Is this high context, or low, and can your problem be solved by fitting your exposition more closely to the context? Are your characters telling themselves or others things they already know, and can you give them a reason to do so? Would they really notice the scenery in this detail? Many, many times an exposition problem can be resolved by considering the context.

Once you've started writing, you're bound to encounter a moment when you can't quite think of the word you want, but don't want to lose your momentum (or forget the rest of the sentence). At that point, you can either keep worrying at the problem, or put something not quite right into the sentence and keep going, planning to go back and find the right word once you've gotten the idea down on paper. One trick I've found useful is to put any second-choice words in square brackets. On a word processor, I can search for the brackets and make sure I've replaced or rethought the words I was unhappy with. When I was working on a typewriter, the brackets (or double parentheses, on my first typewriters) helped me remember to stop and reconsider before I typed that word again in the next draft. You may find it helpful, too, to make a list of potential invented words, so that you can refer to it when you need a new word rather than having to make something up on the spot with no sense of the other words you've used. A friend uses this method in reverse: he keeps a second file open at all times, and each time he makes up a word, copies it to that file. As a result, while he's working, he has a complete list of everything he's already used, and can refer to it for inspiration when he needs to come up with something new. I do similar things with names, both character and place names. At the beginning of the project I make a list that I can refer to when I need it. If the character or place is going to become important to the story, I will use asterisks or ampersands in place of a name until I've made a final decision. I find that having the freedom to go on with the story actually helps me find the words or names more quickly.

Another useful technique, which I learned from my coauthor on *The Armor of Light* and *Point of Hopes*, is to keep a cutting file. No matter how well a manuscript is going, inevitably there comes a time when something good that you've written—the perfect description, a brilliant line of dialogue, whatever—doesn't work where you wrote it. I had been in the habit of swearing a little and then cutting the section (a miserable feeling) or of trying to rewrite it until it fit, or until it became clear that it wasn't going to work in that spot, at which point it had usually lost whatever I'd liked about it in the first place. My coauthor explained that she kept a second file handy on her computer desktop and simply cut the problem section and pasted it into the other one. More often than not, some or all of it could be salvaged for use in a different part of the manuscript. Even when a section wasn't as good as it had looked on first reading, and ultimately was never used, it didn't feel quite as much as though a day's work was being thrown away if it went into the cutting file first.

The point of all of these ideas and suggestions is to get you started and to keep you writing. The biggest problem most would-be writers face is not trying to sell their manuscripts, but finishing one in the first place. If you finish something, be it a novel or a short story, you've already done more and better than most of the people around you. Storytelling is fun; writing—telling stories on paper— can be just as enjoyable, even if the techniques involved require effort to master. After all, this is science fiction: you get not only to tell the story, but also to invent the situation, the world, the characters, and everything that makes it worth telling.

MIND GAMES

1. The Hook: You've heard of a "hooky" song. That's the one you can't get out of your head, that keeps bouncing around in your brain until you go and buy the CD so you can play it again. A common suggestion for opening a novel is to think of a similar hook: some opening that will grab your readers' attention and make them want to sit down right there and read the rest of the novel. (Rachel Pollack's *Temporary Agency* has that quality for me: I was lucky enough to be given a copy by the author, and promptly embarrassed myself by glancing at the first paragraph, and having somebody kick me ten pages later. I was drawn immediately into that world and story.) So, pick an idea and write a single paragraph that will hook your reader into wanting more.

2. High Context/Low Context: (I find this really helpful in smoothing out expository lumps.) Pick one of the crucial ideas or concepts in your story and write a high-context scene between two

(or more, but it's easier with fewer than five) characters involving that idea or concept. Remember, they know what's going on (and so should you). When you're finished, read over it, and, if possible, get someone else who likes SF to read it, too. How much of the scene is comprehensible without additional description? Now write a low-context scene involving the same concept or idea, if possible using one or more of the same characters. How much description did you actually have to add? Which one works better? How easy was it to think of a plausibly low-context situation, and do you want to use anything from that situation in your finished story?

3. Exorcism: If you're really worried about copying a style you've read recently, do it deliberately for a while. Sketch a scene in that voice or style. Often you'll find that it's one facet of the style that's stuck in your head (using present tense, or second person, or an extremely slangy first-person narrator, and so forth), and that may turn out to be something you want to use. It may also turn out, once you've written it out of your system, to be something you want desperately to avoid. Either way, allowing yourself to try the thing you admire gives you the chance to analyze how it works, to see if you can do it, and to decide if any part of it serves the story you want to tell.

4. Voice Exercises: Even if you're pretty sure you know how you want to tell your story, I often find it enlightening to do some sketches in different voices or persons, or from the point of view of characters who will be secondary in the finished book. The latter gives you an outside view of your protagonists, and can be helpful especially if you're working on characters who are going to be misunderstood—you need to be sure it's believable that people react badly to them. The former I find particularly helpful in working out the voices the characters will use in dialogue.

A. How would your characters explain themselves (and/or the events of the story) to a media person? Are they friendly, hostile, willing, unwilling? Do they put themselves forward, or are they embarrassed or diffident—or do they have things to hide? Do they tell stories well, or are they awkward, tongue-tied? Do they use profanity, speak straightforwardly, or choose euphemisms? Do they care what their listener thinks of them? Are they showing off? Try sketching a first-person account of some part of your story, as told to the media.

Try sketching the same incident, but this time as told by the same character to a close friend. How does the character's attitude change? Is he or she more relaxed, or less so? Has he or she more to lose, or more freedom of speech?

An extension provides a good exercise for exploring the low-context/high-context contrast, and for considering the differences between first- and third-person narrative. Try sketching the same encounter a third time, but this time, combine the two, and tell it in the third person rather than in first person. Imagine that two of your characters, who participated in the same incident, are being interviewed together about it. (This doesn't have to be by a media person; the interviewer could be an employer or some other authority figure.) How does the change in voice change the information you can convey, and the way you tell it? Do the characters' voices change depending on who is speaking to whom?

B. Try sketching some interaction between your protagonist and a secondary character, but tell it from the secondary character's point of view. The choice of voice is up to you, but this is a good place to get a handle on what your protagonist looks like, and how other people perceive him or her. (Personally, I find this a good way to spot any overly romanticized vision of a character. That's more likely to come out in my writing in this kind of sketch, and then I've gotten it out of my system, and can guard against it in later work.) Does your protagonist's self-image match other people's perceptions? Who's right? Does your protagonist care?

Interlude

SHAPESHIFTING

THIS EXERCISE WAS SUGGESTED BY REEVES GABRELS'S article, "Fishing with Architecture" in *Guitar for the Practicing Musician*. It's really more a way of limbering up your mind to make the kinds of cross-modal, cross-genre connections that will help you flesh out your worlds and characters, so don't spend too much time on it. (I actually find that this is one way to get myself unstuck in the early stages of a project, by giving me another way to articulate the emotional flavor of a story: should this one feel like Led Zeppelin, or the Cowboy Junkies? Danish Modern or Baroque? An Amish center-diamond quilt, all solid colors, big plain shapes, and elaborate quilting, or a multicolored, multi-pieced, plain-quilted Lone Star quilt?)

1. If your story was an album, what would it be? Would it be classical, baroque, twelve-tone, modal—heavy metal or medieval—cool jazz, or three-chord punk? Chamber music or symphony, or jamfest like the Grateful Dead? A good-time bar band or the Talking Heads? Electric guitar, solo baritone, or drums? Rap or opera? What would the soundtrack of your story sound like? Who would be on it, and are you picking them for lyrics or music?

2. If your story were a building, what sort of architecture would it have? Would it be sleek and modern, heavy Romanesque, or the roccoco wrought iron of New Orleans's Garden District? Would the interior be open-plan, a well-lit loft, or the tiny

rooms and passages of an early modern fortress? Would it be built of stone or wood or steel—or mud brick or hide or woven grass? Is it urban or rural or cheerfully suburban?

You can try this exercise with any other art—painting, sculpture, dance, and so on—that appeals to you, but it works best if you pick something that is not directly narrative. (Drama, for example, doesn't work as well as other arts because, like fiction, it is a story form.) Also, if you enjoy another art or craft, consider how you would express your story through that medium.

9

CHAPTER

Tools of the Trade

HAVING SPENT SO MUCH TIME ON WHAT YOU'RE GOING TO PUT down on paper, it seems worthwhile to spend a little time on how you're likely to do it. In doing so, however, it's important to distinguish between writing your first drafts and completing a version for submission to a publisher. For the first, your own preferences can, and should, guide you; for the second, you have to conform to a standard format. There are also a few tools and techniques you may not have thought of that can prove invaluable in the early stages of a project, and that are worth adopting.

To begin where a project usually begins, I've mentioned my clipping files, and most of you will have at some point encountered the suggestion to keep a journal. The basic concept is to find some format that allows you to record and store stray ideas and bits of writing in some way that will be easily accessible when you need them. Too many people think that they'll remember the gist of an interesting article, or a particularly nice turn of phrase, only to discover too late that they cannot remember the details or even enough context to retrieve the information. The classic solution to this problem is the writer's journal—a notebook of some kind, often loose-leaf, that writers carry with them at all times—but the only thing that's really necessary is some consistent way of recording your ideas. I don't keep a formal journal. I do keep a small notebook in my briefcase, so that it's with me pretty much any time I leave the house. In my office at home I keep two drawers of a filing cabinet filled with folders, each of which represents a potential project or category. I also keep folders of clippings, which get placed into the appropriate project folder as each idea develops. So, in a sense, I do keep a journal; it's just divided among a number of different locations rather than kept in one notebook. I have illegible handwriting at the best of times (it has a very short half-life of about six months: after that, even I don't know what it says), so anything that goes into my notebook gets transcribed onto the computer and then printed out for storage. If my handwriting were better, I'd probably just file the handwritten notes, but then I'd miss the chance to expand on them as I transcribe them.

Of course, this isn't the only solution. I know one person who keeps a microcassette recorder with him to make verbal memos of ideas or phrases; I know others who wouldn't be caught dead with anything except a cheap notebook from the drugstore tucked into their hip pocket. I have another friend who keeps journal notes in a special section of her Dayrunner, while still another carries his laptop everywhere, and keeps his journal on the hard drive. I know many people who buy special notebooks with attractive covers and expensive paper, paper that takes fountain-pen ink well and feels good under the hand. I have favorite pens that I order specially from my local office-supply store, under the fond illusion that they make it easier to read my writing. (I'm waiting for the true palm-sized computer—with keyboard.) The point is to find something that you like and that you can realistically keep with you most (ideally all) of the time. The playwright and teacher of writing Louis Catron actually made one of the first exercises in *Writing, Producing, and Selling Your Play* the purchase and organization of a journal, and it's an excellent idea. Give yourself a week to check not just office-supply stores, though they're the best place to start, but stationery shops and any other place that has writing material (lots of stores carry fancy notebooks or blank books, which may turn out to be right for you). By the end of the seven days, buy yourself something to travel with and establish a journal. It will become the core of your writing life.

The great advantage to a journal is that it makes you write. Even if all you've done is jot down notes about an article you read, or the lyrics of a song you heard, you've written something, and the more you write, the easier the process becomes. This is also a kind of writing that makes self-censorship much harder: after all, these are just notes, rough ideas, small sketches that you can rework later. You can store exercise writing with your notes as well—things you wrote in response to the mind games in this book, for example—and unfinished scenes that you don't know how to resolve. The more material you store in your journal, whether it's the single loose-leaf notebook recommended by Catron, a set of files in a cabinet, or a hierarchy of folders on a computer's hard drive, the more choices you will have when you sit down to construct an idea.

Once you begin writing, whether you're just sketching (my term for the kinds of short scenes that may or may not belong in a completed manuscript, but that help you develop voice, character, and so on) or actually working on a draft of your story, you're again faced with a choice of tools. The most common are pencil (or pen) and paper, the typewriter, and a word processing program, though I have heard of writers who dictate their first drafts into a tape recorder. All of these have advantages and disadvantages, and in the end the choice is completely up to you. Whatever makes you most comfortable—whatever lets you get your words down onto paper with the minimum of interference between your brain and the page—will work at this stage. That said, however, if you really have no idea which method will work best for you, you should try all of them: you may discover something that is genuinely perfect for you.

Pen and paper offer some unique advantages. Many writers find it less intimidating to begin their drafts in longhand. The resulting manuscript isn't printed pages, and therefore doesn't look like a book. They feel more free to make changes in that form than they would if they were facing typed or printed pages. Some people also like the relatively slow pace of writing in longhand. Their hands and brain move at the same speed; as they are concentrating on writing one sentence, in other words, their subconscious is free to invent the next one. Corrections are less intimidating, and can be slipped in as needed. Equally important, you don't need a lot of equipment to write this way, so you can work whenever and wherever you can snatch the time. On the other hand, a manuscript in longhand has to be turned into a printed manuscript at some point before it can be submitted, either by you or someone you pay to type it for you, and that can be both time-consuming and expensive.

Other writers compose at the typewriter, though these days many of them have switched over to the computer and word processor. Ironically, the major reason many people gave for switching to the word processor—ease of correction—is a reason that others remain at their trusty typewriters. Word processors, they feel, permit changes to be made *too* easily, without due time for reflection; worse than that, they encourage sloppy writing by allowing writers to put down placeholder phrases, which are intended to be temporary but which never actually get corrected. For these writers, the discipline imposed by the typewriter—small corrections require messy interlining, and large corrections require retyping entire pages—forces them to make sure that every word they type is carefully chosen, and as close to right as they can get. Too, the exercise of retyping the entire manuscript so that it can be submitted to a publisher allows a writer the chance to see the entire story as a whole. (It also helps catch things like overusing certain words or phrases—problems that are very hard to see during the writing process.) Each of these advantages, however, can just as easily be seen as a disadvantage. For every person who complains about word processors creating sloppy writing, there is another who writes more fluidly knowing that his choices aren't fixed in stone, and that anything can be altered with a few keystrokes. The final revision that one person achieves by laboriously retyping a 350-page manuscript is achieved by someone else through careful rereading and a day at the keyboard. It's ultimately a matter of individual temperament.

The computer running a word processing program is probably the most common way to write these days. The advantages, as stated above, are ease of revision—no more ugly typos (you should have seen what this line looked like a moment ago), and no awkward interlined paragraphs, or extra sheets of paper with arrows indicating the proper insertion point. Word processing proponents argue that the ease of correction, rather than encouraging sloppy writing, allows writers to spend more time revising their work. If a last-minute decision to revise Chapter 2 no longer means retyping it and all the subsequent chapters, they say, writers are more likely to make those changes. It's also possible to type far faster on a computer keyboard than on a mechanical typewriter, even an electric one; the keys or typeball could move only so fast, and set a physical limit on the speed at which you could get the words down without tangling the mechanism.

The disadvantages are the ones stated above—it is possible to get lazy and fail to make intended corrections, or (more commonly) to spend so much time revising the little things that there's no time left to give a manuscript a last comprehensive revision. Also, no one word processing program is perfect: for one thing, none of them was written with creative writers in mind, and the things that are absolutely vital for a business writer, or a secretary, are often useless to writers of fiction. For example, spell-check programs that beep every time you misspell a word will also try to correct any invented terms you use. And how often do you see footnotes in fiction? Different programs have different features, and you may find yourself buying a lot of things you don't want in order to get one or two things that you really need. It's helpful to give some thought to your working habits before you go shopping for a word processing program. Do you use a lot of accents and diacritical marks, or complex typography? Then you need a program that will make it easy for you to access accents and to redefine keystrokes so that a simple combination will trigger special characters. I find that having keyboard equivalents to most mouse commands comes in really handy when I'm in the middle of a thought and don't want to take my hand off the keyboard. A key command that puts the cursor back to its previous position is a wonderful luxury that my current program doesn't have. I also like to be able to type in small capital letters, though that's not actually that important. Once you've made some lists of what you're looking for, try to find a store that lets you test drive the program first. (A music store lets you play the instruments before you commit to one of them, right? You're probably spending about the same amount of money.) The good news is that it's hard to go too far wrong, given the programs that are on the market right now. All of them will let you produce a perfectly acceptable manuscript, and that's all you really need.

The other important part of a computer/word processor system is the printer. You have to have a machine that will produce clear, crisp black print on plain white paper—no fuzzy edges, no smearing, no wavering. After all, eventually editors are going to read the output from this machine, and you want them to have a favorable impression from the start, not to be squinting and straining over poor print. These days, it's almost impossible to find the old dot matrix systems, at least new, though if you buy a used system, you may run into one now and then. If you're considering one, be sure and test its "best" print quality: if you can see dots at all, it's not worth it. The other choices are basically ink-jet printer, laser printers, and service bureaus. Ink-jets are cheap, though the ink cartridges are moderately expensive, but their output is slow, only a few pages per minute. Also, the ink is water soluble, and can smear badly if it gets wet. Laser printers are expensive, though the prices have dropped significantly over the last few years, and the cost of toner and other supplies can be prohibitive. Laser printers are fast, however; their output is consistently very good, and they are designed to stand up under constant, professional use. If you can afford one, that's probably the way to go. On the other hand, ink-jet printers produce perfectly adequate manuscripts for a very reasonable cost. This is one of many places where time can substitute for money: you can avoid spending large sums of money on a laser printer by budgeting and spending several extra days on the final printing. You can also take a disk containing your manuscript to one of the many service bureaus that offer printing from disk, and have them print it out for you. These bureaus tend to have the best laser printers available to them, but they're correspondingly expensive—and you have to be sure your disk is in a format their computers can read. However, these places can be a lifesaver in the event of a printer problem.

One final advantage to the computer is that it can do more than just run a word processor. Software stores and catalogs are full of programs that claim to help organize your work, or to provide a space within which inspiration can strike. With a modem, you can connect to the Internet and World Wide Web or to any number of on-line services. The utility of all these things is largely a personal matter. Some people swear by specific outlining or creativity programs, while others swear at them. For example, I find a program called Three by Five extremely useful. It is marketed as a screenwriter's tool, and is set up as the virtual analog of pinning index-card notes to a corkboard, but it also allows the cards to be tied to each other in complex ways, and to be sorted as though they were entries in a database. Some variation of this method—shuffling notes according to different criteria—has always worked for me; the software lets me do it better than I could before. People who don't find the method terribly useful to begin with would find the software to be a waste of money. In general, then, if you're looking for software tools, I would suggest looking for programs that let you do something that you either already do or would do if you'd been able to figure out a way to do it on paper. A program that offers you new ways to do something you'd never really thought about doing should be approached with caution, and tried out extensively before you buy it.

Personally, I work on a computer, with a word processor and several other software tools installed. I've mentioned Three by Five, which I use for plotting and for things like designing complex systems. I also have a complete set of Internet access software, and have set up personalized news services on a couple of the major search engines. I have an encyclopedia and an almanac on CD-ROM for quick and basic reference work. (And, of course, I have several versions of Solitaire for times when the writing is going less than well.) I use a Macintosh because the graphic interface fits the way I think and because I find the Mac system more intuitively obvious than Windows. I know other people who love Windows, or even straight MS-DOS, and I even have one friend who genuinely prefers the power and complexity of a Unix box. (She considers me a techno-wimp for owning a Mac.) What matters is to take the time to discover the tools and methods that work for you. At the first-draft stage, and until you're actually ready to submit a manuscript, your preferences and idiosyncrasies are your own business. Do what works for you, and don't let anybody tell you otherwise.

When it comes to passing your words on to somebody else—preferably an editor who can publish them—things change. You cannot submit a handwritten manuscript. No professional editor or agent will read it, and attempting to submit one will only annoy the other person and stigmatize you as an amateur and someone who couldn't be bothered to find out about the minimum professional standards. Your manuscript has to be printed, or typed, and it has to be in as clean a form as possible. These days, with the proliferation of personal computers, editors are likely to be less tolerant of interlined corrections or white-out than they used to be. No matter how much they recognize the difference between a typed manuscript and a computer printout, they will be inclined, quite unconsciously, to see a typed manuscript with corrections as less finished. Still, if you're a good enough typist, or if you can afford to hire one, a typewritten manuscript is perfectly acceptable. It's probably worth your while, however, to learn how to type, or at least to hunt and peck efficiently and accurately. The ideal situation is to reach a point at which the time you spend preparing your manuscript for submission is worth less—costs less, in other words—than the fee you would pay a professional to do it for you. Your typing skills, of course, will carry over to the computer keyboard, and speed up both creative work and the work of preparing a manuscript. Don't use script, headline, or fancy display fonts, even in headers, and make sure the output is crisp and easy to read. If you feel you have to use a nonstandard character or a standard character in an unfamiliar way, think twice. If there's a way that you can achieve your goal without using unfamiliar elements, do it. You don't want your typography to distract from your story. If you absolutely cannot find a way around it, then include a cover sheet with the manuscript explaining what you've done.

The manuscript should be typed double-spaced and on one side of the paper only. You should use black print on white paper, and you should leave one-inch margins on each edge. (This isn't anal; this is trying to make your work as easy to read as possible.) You should number the pages consecutively rather than by chapter, and you should put an identifier at the top of each page so that if your manuscript and four others get knocked off your editor's desk, yours can be reassembled easily. For many years, I used the working title as the identifier, until my agent asked me to stop. He pointed out that if an editor absolutely hates the working title, which happens and not always for good reason, seeing that title at the top of each and every page will not increase that editor's good feeling toward the book. Now I just use my last name and the page number as the header. If you're working on a word processor, avoid using the various fancy styles like boldface and shadow or outline type; many editors prefer to see underlining in place of italics, so you can't go wrong with that.

A few publishers are starting to ask for manuscripts on disk, but this usually comes after the manuscript has been bought and scheduled for publication. The typesetter then works from your disk, or a translation, depending on format, thus saving the time and money usually spent keying the entire manuscript into the typesetter's system. (Ironically, no SF publisher that I've worked with does; the publisher of this book is the first.) If you end up at a publisher that wants disks, your editor will tell you the formats they can accept and any special requirements before you turn in the final version.

Your tools have to do two things for you: first, they have to give you the freedom to play, to brainstorm, to get words down on paper and to tell your stories as painlessly as possible. Second, they have to allow you to put those stories into a form that is suitable for submission to a publisher. Techniques that work for your friends may not work for you; spend some time trying out a few of the various methods that I've mentioned, or that you hear about from other people, and see what makes you feel best. The only thing that's fixed is the form of a submitted manuscript. For the rest, it's your choice, your taste, your preferences, and your idiosyncrasies.

10

CHAPTER

Moving On

WRITING IS NOT SOMETHING THAT YOU LEARN AND THEN continue doing in the same way for the rest of your career. Rather, it is (or should be) an ongoing process, with each new project offering a fresh set of challenges, something new to learn. (If this sounds as though I'm saying that every time you overcome one problem, learn to do one thing well, something else appears that you have to learn. . . . well, yes. But that's the good part.) Seriously, each new project offers you new chances to grow in your craft; each finished book, I find, shows me things I can do better. This is not to say that I'm dissatisfied with the work I've done, but rather that finishing one project seems to lead to new ideas and new techniques that I want to try. Because writing is a process as well as a discrete set of projects, however, I'd like to consider where you can go after you finish your first project, or your fifth, or your hundredth.

The biggest temptation for any writer is to stop reading. Genre writers, it seems, are particularly prone to a syndrome in which we stop reading other writing in our field, even though we still love the field and are continuing to work in it. Often this stems from simple lack of time: professional reading time gets spent on nonfiction, as we research the next book. By the time we snatch a few minutes to read for pleasure, we are too tired to give genre books the attention they deserve. Instead, we turn to something else—a different genre, maybe, or more general fiction—promising ourselves that we'll read those books later, when we're more awake. Then the Hugo or

Nebula ballot crosses our desks, and we realize with a sinking feeling that we haven't read half the nominees. Sometimes it's for fear that we'll be too influenced by someone else's vision of the same topic, particularly in the early stages of an idea. It's not an unreasonable concern, either, particularly when you're reading good writers; nonetheless, there is so much SF being published that there's usually something out there that you're not working on.

The first reason that it's so important to keep reading is to keep in touch with the field. I'm only in part talking about keeping abreast of hot trends or quick-moving opportunities. As mentioned previously, SF is in some ways a long, complex conversation among writers and readers—this is one of the reasons that it's important to become familiar with the field before trying to write in it. You're stepping into an ongoing dialogue, and if you're merely repeating something someone else has said, or, worse, doing so without realizing it, your potential peers are likely to tune you out. This obligation to stay in touch doesn't end with your first sale. It's vital to stay up on the conversation, even if you decide not to participate in a particular hot subject or subgenre. It's important to maintain the connection, to remain part of the community. Writing is not, despite the romantic image of writers toiling endlessly in a lonely garret, a particularly solitary profession. You need contact with other people not only to keep you inspired and excited about what you do, but also to develop and maintain a professional standing. Reading other people's work is an important step in that process.

The second reason to keep reading is that reading other people's writing is one of the best and easiest ways to learn craft and art, and that learning continues lifelong. By looking at other people's work, even and maybe especially styles and topics that are very different from the ones you normally choose, you can learn a lot about how novels can be constructed. You may not choose to employ all or even most of the techniques you study, or you may modify them to your needs, but by considering them you will have learned something about how you choose to write. One way I've found to make myself read more widely than I might otherwise is to do book reviews. Because I am assigned or choose books according to the publication's needs, I pick from a different group than I would necessarily select for pleasure reading, and the needs of the review format force me to assess the book both as a reader and as a writer. After all, I may not like a particular book, but have to admit that it's a classic example of its genre—and can recommend it on those grounds. If you can teach yourself to think on both levels, personal and professional, you'll be able to judge a work both on its own terms, the framework within which its author was working, and on your own. It's a matter of learning the difference between your personal taste and the requirements of any particular genre, and learning how to respect genres without compromising your own integrity as a writer.

Beyond the relatively simple matter of learning to read fairly, within the author's intent as well as from your own perspective, there is the question of text and subtext (assumptions authors make about the way their world works, about the way people work). Just because a work is genre fiction doesn't mean it has no subtext. All authors have their own worldviews, and those views tend to be revealed in their fiction, simply because most authors write about matters that concern them deeply. On the other hand, not all authors choose to concern themselves with subtext, feeling either that it is by definition outside their control, or that it's an inappropriate concern for writers of purely recreational fiction. The latter is hard to accept if you have any ambition to be a serious writer, or if you take science fiction at all seriously—and if you don't, why are you writing it? The former has more merit: subtext is generally accepted to be something formed at a subconscious level, and it is difficult to hold an artist accountable for inadvertent decisions. Nor is it fully fair to assume that you know anything about a writer's personal beliefs outside the particular context of the novel. Science fiction, after all, is built on extreme situations and exaggerations, which the writer may use without believing in their intrinsic merit. Readers' individual interpretations of subtext are also influenced by their own experiences. Nonetheless, becoming aware of subtext will help give you an increased understanding of yourself and your own writing. It will certainly help you to ask yourself whether you like a book because or in spite of its subtext.

Whether or not you choose to consider subtext (though I hope you will), analyzing what you like and dislike in other people's writing will help you build your own craft. On the most basic level, everybody learns by imitation. When you read a particularly effective scene, take a minute to analyze what makes it so effective. Is it a flowing stream of language that carries you through essentially improbable events? Is there a single, perfectly chosen detail that would never have occurred to you, but that brings the situation into sharp and sudden focus? Does the author's way of handling dialogue make the characters' voices ring true? Is there a particularly clever method for slipping exposition into the story? Whatever it is that catches your attention, it may be something you can learn to do. This may not be possible, at least not the way your models are doing it: some writers' styles are so seamless and unique that imitation proves very difficult. However, by figuring out what these writers are doing, and trying to achieve a similar effect yourself (even if you have to go about it an entirely different way because of the nature of your story or simply the limits of your taste and ability), you've taken the first step toward developing a voice and style of your own.

You can also learn by avoidance. When you read something you don't like, or that doesn't work for you, take a few minutes to analyze what went wrong between the author's intention and your brain. (For me, this is often signaled by a kind of mental "clunk" that jolts me out of the process of the story.) Why is there an expository lump here, and how else could the information have been presented? What makes you so sure that character would never behave that way, or say that sentence? Why doesn't this bit of extrapolation work for you? (If, as is often the case, it's because you know more than the author does about a particular subject, you've just had an object lesson in the importance of solid research.) In its most dramatic form, this kind of learning takes the form of the statement, "I can do better than that" or "If they'll publish this, they'll publish me." This is a perfectly reasonable place to start, as long as you remember that you thought your inspiration was pretty bad. You *can* do better than that, and you should certainly try.

Once you have the basic skills down, you need to learn to make each part of your story support the others, and make each of them serve your overall vision of the story. This can be like juggling in zero-gravity: as you work on each part individually, it's easy to forget the other parts, and to get carried away with a clever idea. When the story is put back together, that clever idea then unbalances the story you wanted to tell, tipping in an entirely different direction. At that point, you can either run with it, making the changes you need, or rein in the clever idea, reserving it for another story. This isn't particularly easy to do, but sometimes it's necessary to preserve the story you really wanted to tell. For example, I had a wonderful idea for a new form of FTL drive when I was working on *Burning Bright*, and did quite a bit of note taking and sketching on that system. However, when I actually started writing the novel, I discovered that adding any of those details distracted from the Game that had to be the center of the story. I ended up cutting most of the details I'd put in—I did save them, and hope to use them in a different novel some day where they can get the play they deserve—but it made *Burning Bright* a better, tighter, and more consistent novel. On the other hand, Ursula K. Le Guin's "The Shobies' Story," which appears in her collection *A Fisherman of the Inland Sea*, is a truly beautiful example of all the parts serving the whole. The premise of the story—the development and first human-crewed test of the *churten* drive, which allows instantaneous travel from one place to another—turns out to hinge on the ability to tell a story. Everything from the title to the conversational, deceptively simple language, to the climactic image with its deliberate echo of Plato's story of the cave, to the final line ("And the Shobies looked at one another and said, 'Well, it's quite a story. . . .' ") was carefully chosen to reinforce the reader's understanding of that single idea.

A final way to grow as a writer is to do your best to push yourself, to try to stretch your personal limits with each story you do. This is risky business, of course—the chance of failure is higher when you're trying something new, reaching for something that has been a little bit beyond you—but with each attempt, whether or not it's fully successful, you will have learned a little bit more. It's also risky because you're asking yourself constantly to reevaluate your beliefs as well as your writing strategies, to say to yourself, "Is this a story I want to tell?" as well as "Is this a story I can tell?" You may not choose to take all risks at the same time. For example, you might select a story with characters that you find comfortable and easy to write when you want to work on exposition or plot, or stick to a style and voice you know you can do when you choose a topic that challenges you. Sometimes you may opt simply to consolidate your gains, to tell a story that stretches you just a little in several different directions, and sometimes you may come up against an idea that you can't leave alone that forces you to make several major leaps all at once. The important thing, however, is to be willing to take these chances as they arise. Without that willingness, you risk staying the same, repeating essentially the same story until you yourself are tired of it.

At the same time, you can't stop doing the kind of research I recommended in Chapters 2 and 7. In fact, you should probably continually expand, if not the research itself, then at least your consciousness of potential "what ifs." The more times you stop and ask yourself that question, whether it's about an article you've read or a passing remark overheard in a crowd, the more possibilities open up to you. You should definitely keep some kind of record of those ideas—the journal is an obvious way to do it, in whatever form seems most congenial to you—and you should review that record as often as possible. You never know what half-forgotten fragment of information will fit perfectly into an existing idea. Continue to cultivate serendipity, to put yourself into situations where you are likely to come into contact with new ideas, people, and information. Observe the people around you, take a different road home, take a class in a subject that interests you, but make sure you keep in touch with the world outside science fiction's narrow limits.

More than that, once you have an idea, you need to remember to ask the hard questions, rather than stopping at the easy or obvious answers. How far can you push your "what if"? Does its logical extreme scare or upset you? Would it make a good story anyway? If you want to explore contemporary issues through a science fictional disguise, be sure you understand both sides' arguments even when you passionately disagree with one of them. Ask yourself what will happen ten, twenty, fifty years after the events of your story: are the long-term consequences of your "what if" potentially more interesting than its discovery?

It's also important to remember that science, despite its real attempts at objectivity, is in practice a social activity. That is to say, scientists are members of society, and share its assumptions about the way the world should function. In fact, assumptions about the way the world does function are often conditioned—framed, if you will—by assumptions about the way things should be. This is not to argue that science is necessarily flawed, nor to say that the self-correcting mechanisms built into the practice do not (in general) function properly, but to point out that society's deep concerns influence which problems are seen as important and worthy of study. Thus, nineteenth-century scientists, preoccupied with hierarchies of race, spent a great deal of time trying to determine which measurement of man gave the most "accurate" (i.e., the most in conformity with their assumptions about the relationship between race and status) ranking of the human species. (I recommend Stephen J. Gould's *The Mismeasure of Man*, Carol Tavris's *The Mismeasure of Woman*, and Anne Fausto-Sterling's *Myths of Gender* for examples of the ways that contemporary concerns influence and sometimes distort scientific objectivity.) For example, medieval and early modern scientists found numerous examples of higher sex drive in women, operating from a model that presumed women were generally more lustful than men. By the nineteenth century, however, as women were presumed to be more pure than men, and a purifying influence on them, scientists discovered evidence that proved that truly womanly women were essentially uninterested in sex. It's important, too, to keep in mind the relationship between scientific and political metaphor. Louis XI could not have called himself "The Sun King"—that phrase was meaningless in a geocentric universe. But Louis XIV, operating in a heliocentric world, found it to be a tremendously potent metaphor. Similarly, the declaration of a "war on cancer" produced a different attitude toward research (and toward its successes and failures) than the various attempts to "solve the puzzle" of AIDS.

I'd also encourage you to write in more than one universe. I'm well aware that there are plenty of highly successful writers who invent a universe that appeals to them and then spend most of their careers describing the adventures of a limited set of favorite characters in that setting. However, if you look more closely at those writers, you'll usually find that even people as closely identified with a particular series as, say, Piers Anthony, Marion Zimmer

Bradley, or Anne McCaffrey have also written (and published) books that aren't part of their most famous series. These other works have not been as successful, certainly from a commercial and arguably from an artistic standpoint (though I actually prefer McCaffrey's non-Pern stories), but I suspect that these stories are really important to the writers.

Why? After all, as I've already established, building a convincing universe is hard work, and peopling it with interesting characters is even harder. Why do it a second time, or more, when you've got a setting that works and characters you know and love? First, part of being an SF writer is creating new worlds, and you need to keep those skills sharp. It's a simple question of technique: if you don't practice your craft, you don't learn anything new, and world and character building are vital parts of the craft of SF. Second, if you grow at all as a writer, you're going to wish you had made different choices, and other universes allow you to try those out as well. Third—and this is something mystery writers know and deal with even more than SF writers—the series format is subtly different from a stand-alone novel, and requires different goals and choices.

Wanting new choices is actually the reason I don't do series SF much myself. When I wrote *Five-Twelfths of Heaven*, I—foolishly— didn't see it as the first book in a series, and steamed ahead with the narrative without considering the long-range implications of a number of things I threw in to describe character or setting. I mentioned a matriarchal planet, which later contradicted a universe of absolute patriarchy that I needed for the second and third books. I didn't know where Earth was, or how the characters were going to get there, although that was the ostensible focus of the story, and so by the time I got to the third book, which resolved that question, I'd inadvertently set things up so that the neatest solution I could think of would have flatly contradicted the science in the first book. Finally, as I've mentioned before (see Chapter 8), I gave the main character, Silence Leigh, a personality trait that proved to be totally inappropriate and inconvenient for the rest of the series. By making her uncomfortable around the homunculi that functioned as robots in this society, I was able to have her describe the first one she encountered in necessary detail. In the later books, when

Silence discovered her talents and became the first woman magus her society had ever encountered, this dislike became a real nuisance. By the third book, *The Empress of Earth*, there were several problems that could most easily have been resolved by Silence's growing a homunculus—a skill I had not established that she had, and that contradicted a basic and important personality trait already established.

Could all of this have been solved by better planning? Most certainly—but that level of planning was completely beyond my ability at that point in my career. With practice, you learn why you make certain choices, as well as how you make them. Before that time, you're more likely to make decisions that come back to haunt you later on, and a series, in which the basic parameters are set in the first novel, just compounds the problem. It is possible to rearrange your series world by authorial fiat—Marion Zimmer Bradley did just that in her Darkover novels—but, to put it bluntly, you need to be as popular as Bradley to get away with it. It is better to take what you've learned from your early work and apply that knowledge to something new that can be shaped the way you want from the start. And then, of course, you do it all again as you outgrow the constraints of that universe.

The final problem with series writing is produced by the structural difference between a series and a stand-alone novel. One of the basic assumptions of the novel is that the events it describes are the most important ones in the lives of the main characters. (If they aren't, why bother writing about them?) A series novel flatly contradicts this: if there are more novels coming, clearly some of these characters are going to be around for the sequels, and that means that *this* novel isn't necessarily where the big events are happening. A finite series (a trilogy or its relatives) has fewer problems with this than unbounded series such as Jeff Carver's Infinite Sea stories, or Lois McMasters Bujold's Miles Voskorsigan novels, or any series mystery. The events of a trilogy can be assumed to be the focus of the characters' lives, and it's possible that no one will survive the end of the final book. At the same time, it's still harder to structure each part of a finite series so that it is individually satisfying. (Yes, some people don't and get away with it: each book of Roger

Zelazny's Amber series ended with a cliff-hanger, and readers waited a year or more to find out what happened in the next volume, but this really wasn't playing fair. More to the point, I'm not the only person who stopped buying the books and checked them out of the library instead.) This is the reason for the "second-book doldrums" or its cousin, the "second-book bloodies." In the first case, the events of the middle novel are crucial, but they have neither the freshness of the first novel or the satisfaction of the story's climax to carry the readers along; by comparison, the second novel seems a little dull. The "second-book bloodies" is a common way of avoiding the doldrums: kill something, or a lot of somethings, so that vivid action carries the reader through the second book to the real climax in the third.

An unbounded series has the same problems to a much larger degree: most of them are carried by a single popular protagonist (think about how many of these series are known by the protagonist's name) and therefore you know that each individual novel cannot be the most important event of the eponymous protagonist's life. More important, that protagonist can't change too much, or you risk disappointing the very readers who have made the character popular.

There are solutions, of course. Bujold and McCaffrey, for example, have established large (and growing) casts of characters, and switch points of view among them. (This is the way some of the best mystery writers handle a problem that is even more common in their genre, and if you're contemplating this kind of unbounded series, you'd do well to read mysteries to see some other ways that the structure can be handled.) In this case, part of the pleasure of reading the series is in seeing each familiar character from a new perspective, and that becomes as important as the events of the novel. Carver's Infinite Sea novels are rooted in a premise that allows him to take his protagonists from one world to another, so that they are not only trying to solve their personal dilemmas but also struggling repeatedly in dangerous and potentially disastrous situations. These situations *are* the most important events in the lives of the secondary characters, and the protagonists must help resolve them in order to survive themselves. Another option is to keep raising the stakes, so that the events of each novel are, at that moment, the most important events in the protagonists' lives. Unfortunately, you're likely to run out of options pretty quickly: after your hero has saved the universe once, what do you do for an encore? Finding a bigger menace only works for so long. . . . Finally there is the technically challenging method of letting your protagonist grow with you, hoping that she doesn't change so much that she no longer fits the universe you created or confuses the readers who are only just discovering your first books. However, the basic structure of a series—the promise a series makes to the reader—suggests that the novels within it will be more alike than they are different, and that is a very good way to burn out and become bored with your own work. If you have other universes in mind, it is a good idea to explore them and work on a different set of problems. Then, if you choose, you can come back to your original series refreshed and remembering what it was you loved about it in the first place.

My final message here is to remind you that writing matters. It matters because art matters, because storytelling matters—because the stories we tell define us as a culture, and because our stories are a way of communicating with other people. I'm not just talking about much-maligned subtext; in some ways, that's always beyond our control, though maybe not as much as some critics would have us believe. Rather, I'm talking about the text itself, about the surface of the story as well as its implications. It's important to be aware of our own assumptions and prejudices, and to acknowledge them if you choose not to overset them—in other words, to be sure you mean what you say and say what you mean.

This is always easier to see in someone else's work—a novel based on a premise that you find repugnant, or making assumptions about society that you emphatically disbelieve. Our own assumptions always seem more like self-evident truth, particularly if, like most of us, you move in circles that basically confirm your views. Nonetheless, your beliefs can't help influencing your fiction, and if you are honest with yourself and your readers, you will acknowledge that fact. This doesn't mean that everything you write will be a campaign piece for some cause you believe in—polemics aren't fiction—or that there's anything wrong with letting your beliefs influence your fiction. In fact, quite the opposite is true:

Louis Catron argues in *Writing, Producing, and Selling Your Play* that his students should begin by identifying the things that they feel and believe most strongly, and, while I wouldn't go that far before writing a novel, I think that a passionate interest or belief is vital to making any piece of fiction live. So long as you remember that you are writing fiction, with all its ambiguities, letting your beliefs influence your writing is hardly a problem.

A different problem does arise, however, when someone—a friend, an editor, a reader—calls you on what you've written. When someone approaches you at a convention, scowling, and offers some variation on the statement, "I can't believe *you* would write something like this," it's hard to know how to respond. For that matter, it is distressing when a reviewer recognizes your beliefs, disagrees with them, and responds to your book on that basis rather than on the merits of the story. Particularly if you've never given the matter a thought—if no one who's seen the manuscript ever mentioned what they saw in it, or if they simply agreed with you—this can be a very jarring moment. It's bad enough when someone doesn't like your work; when they not only dislike what you've done, but pull out from it ideas that you believe in and hold them up to disapproval or ridicule, it's even more painful. At that point, it's easy to retreat to a defensive posture: "What's the matter with you? It's only a story. Lighten up!" (Or, "Get a sense of humor!") But the minute you say that it's only a story, that it doesn't count—that you don't set value on your own work—you lose the chance to defend yourself and your work on its own terms. Even a story that was written for fun, to be enjoyed as a good read, deserves to be taken seriously on its own terms. You deserve to take yourself seriously enough to know what you mean, and to say it clearly. That knowledge not only makes for a better book, but also can prove an excellent armor against critics or negative reviews. If nothing else, knowing what you meant makes it easier to spot the reviewer or reader who didn't like your work solely because they didn't agree with your perspective. More than that, being aware of what you believe and the ways that you express your values in your work ultimately helps you improve the work. Whether I or anyone agrees with you is less important than becoming better at what you do.

II
PART

WRITING AS PROFESSION

11
CHAPTER

Starting Out

ONE PIECE OF RECEIVED WISDOM IN SCIENCE FICTION IS THAT aspiring writers should begin with short fiction, perhaps even make a few sales to the magazines, and only then tackle something as ambitious as a novel. On the one hand, the idea has some merit. This is the way most of the Golden Age writers learned their craft, and short stories are (in theory, at least) somewhat easier to write and to sell. There are four or five major magazines, and dozens of minor ones, all of which need material on a regular basis. It is also somewhat easier to approach an agent or an editor for a novel if you can point to one or two short story sales. After all, they think, other people have thought your work was good enough to pay for it. On the other hand, short stories and novels are very different in structure and tone. Some writers who are brilliant at short fiction can't sustain that pitch for the length of a novel; others (myself among them) can't move from the comfortable space of a novel to the tight focus of a short story. If you can do both, and if you enjoy writing short fiction, selling a short story or two first will probably help you some in selling a novel. If you don't like or want to write short stories, however, you don't have to do it. Not having short fiction sales won't keep you from selling a novel, and if your most natural length is the novel, you shouldn't try to force yourself into short fiction.

A related question is whether or not there is some formal course of study that will help make you a writer. Personally, I think that the best preparation is probably some form of the classic liberal arts education—a program that makes you read and think and write, and encourages you to explore a number of topics and interests without considering whether or not they prepare you for a real-world job. If you're interested in science fiction, it seems logical to major in one of the sciences, but actually I think your subject of study is largely irrelevant as long as it interests and challenges you. I was a historian; some of my close friends were mathematicians, English majors, French majors, and, of course, the inevitable computer science major. It's more important to learn how to learn, and how to go on learning after graduation, than to digest a set of facts that will inevitably become obsolete.

That said, it's vital that you take enough science courses to understand the grammar of the scientific method. The specific facts are less important than learning how science is done: how questions are formulated, how experiments are developed, and how theories are proposed. Without an understanding of the scientific paradigms and method, you won't be able to formulate the kinds of "what ifs" that make for good science fiction. Starhawk's The Fifth Sacred Thing is a good example: the novel borrows many of the elements of classic science fiction—the post-holocaust setting, the struggling survivors caught between natural forces and an invading power, and so on—but both the basic premise and the resolution are based on essentially religious assumptions, which by definition are not falsifiable and therefore outside the realm of science.

There are, of course, programs that allow you to major in creative writing, but I'm personally wary of them. Most beginning writers lack not only the self-knowledge to be able to assess their own work fairly but also the self-confidence to stand up to criticism that may be completely wrong. Beyond that, however, I feel that majoring in creative writing focuses a writer too narrowly, shutting him off from a wider range of experience before he has had a chance to explore more than a few possibilities. Formal workshops present some of the same problems. A stint at Clarion (the major SF writing program) or one of its cousins may well help you get an editor to look at your work more quickly. You may also learn quite a bit about craft from your fellow students and from the writers who teach there. To get the most out of the workshops, however, you need a certain level of experience so that you can analyze what you're being told and see if it is right for you. You also need the self-confidence to be able to handle that level of criticism, and that, too, tends to come from experience. I really believe that workshops are far more useful for writers who already have some idea of what they want to say, and of how they want to say it, than for people who are just beginning to explore their interests.

The first real step toward becoming a professional writer is to finish something. That may seem obvious beyond belief, but actually producing a completed manuscript puts you well ahead of the majority of people who say, vaguely, "I think I want to be a writer." The second step is to submit that manuscript to a publisher or an agent. Again, that should seem obvious, but many would-be writers, once they've finished a manuscript, get cold feet at the idea of submitting it for the professional-level criticism that accompanies offering it for sale. It can be an intimidating process to go from the generally supportive atmosphere of friends and writing groups to the impersonal world of form rejection letters and four-month turn-arounds. However, if you don't brave that world, take that risk, there is no chance at all that your work will be published, and thus no chance for people to read the story you have to tell. And that, ultimately, defeats the real purpose of writing: telling your stories to other people.

Selling a novel is, in theory at least, a basically straightforward process. You the writer select a publisher who publishes the kind of material you write, and if possible find within that house an editor who actually acquires books like the ones you write—not necessarily the same subgenre, but novels with the same sensibility and/or level of ambition. Then check one of the numerous directories to find out what that publisher's submission policy is. (If necessary, ask the publisher directly.) Then do what it says: if they want a query letter, send a query letter. If it's three chapters and an outline, send that. If they want to see the full manuscript, send that. The main issue at this point is not to rule yourself out by doing something annoyingly inappropriate. Then you wait, often for several months. Your manuscript, if you sent one, is now in what's called the slush pile, waiting to be read. After the third month, you can send a follow-up note or postcard, ideally with a stamped, self-addressed envelope (SASE), inquiring as to the status of your manuscript/query/proposal. A couple of weeks later, you will receive your postcard back stating that the manuscript is still under consideration. A few weeks after that, you will get the real answer: acceptance, conditional rejection ("we like parts of this, but can't buy it in its present form; if you wanted to work on it and resubmit it, we'd like to see it"), or rejection.

If the manuscript was rejected, treat yourself to something that will make you feel better. I buy makeup; there is probably something very Freudian there. Then check over any comments from the editor (and if there are any, congratulate yourself: editors rarely have the time to make comments on any manuscript that doesn't have some potential), decide if they have merit and if you want to follow them, and then send the manuscript out again. Find another publisher that looks likely, and repeat the process.

If your manuscript got a conditional rejection, congratulate yourself—if you drink alcohol, a cheap bottle of champagne would not be inappropriate. Allow yourself to appreciate what you've accomplished: an editor has looked at your manuscript, and seen enough merit in it to spend time thinking about what would make it publishable. Then sit down with the editor's comments and give them some serious thought. Are they good suggestions? Did the editor get what you were trying to say, and do the comments help you communicate better? Do they improve the storytelling or the writing? Are they changes you're willing to make? If they aren't, that's your choice, and, depending on the nature of the comments and the requested changes, ignoring them may very well be the best thing you can do. Pick another publisher, and try again.

On the other hand, if the changes make sense to you, and you're willing to do the work "on spec," i.e., without a contract, then get to work. Make the changes, reprint or retype the manuscript, and send it in again, being sure to mention in your cover letter that you are doing this at the editor's suggestion. (Given the turnover in publishing these days, it's probably a good idea to confirm that the editor in question is still at that publisher.) Then the process starts over again. The novel still may not sell—the editor may have changed his or her mind in the intervening time, or may have just bought something too similar, or the way you made the changes may not work for this particular editor, or the editorial committee may overrule the editor—but you've at least made a major step forward.

If the manuscript was accepted, celebrate. Pat yourself on the back, take yourself out for a nice dinner, in general let yourself savor the moment. Then get to work: you have two big tasks in front of you, negotiating the contract, and dealing with any revisions your editor deems necessary and with the rest of the production process before the novel sees print. Contract negotiation is always difficult, particularly for a first-time novelist. If you can get expert help, it's worthwhile to do so—but make sure your advisors are experts in *book* contracts, not general contracts. (Book contracts are like nothing else in the world, and a lawyer whose experience is in other fields will only mess you up.) If you have an agent, follow his or her advice; if you don't, or don't want one, do some homework before signing. The Science Fiction and Fantasy Writers of America has a standard contract containing the provisions that they recommend as a minimum, and you'd be wise to look that over and compare it to the one being offered to you. Even if you can't get everything they suggest, you may be able to get some provisions changed, or percentages adjusted in your favor. The more you know about what is (and isn't) normal, the more likely you are to get what you want without alienating your editor. For more information on contracts and negotiation, it's worth consulting writers' magazines. The SFFWA *Bulletin* has run periodic articles on contracts and negotiating strategies, as well as discussions of the advantages and disadvantages of having an agent; other writers' magazines have done the same. Many other writing books discuss the salient points of a contract as well; of those, Donald Maass's *The Career Novelist* is particularly useful in its realistic discussion of the business side of writing.

Once the contract is signed, a manuscript moves through a standard process that turns it into the bound volume on the bookstore shelves. Although details vary from publisher to publisher, the basic steps remain constant. Readers and first-time authors (and even some experienced writers) often have mistaken ideas of what publishers do, and how long it takes to do it, so it's worth going over the process quickly. First, you must finish any revisions suggested by the editor. This is, of course, open to a certain amount of negotiation, but it doesn't seem smart to sign a contract offered on the basis of revisions you're unwilling to make.

Then the manuscript will be passed on to a copy editor for further revision. The copy editor's job is to check for consistency—of grammar, usage, invented terms and spellings, and anything else that may have been overlooked by the author. Copy editors will also query anything that they find confusing, and pass the manuscript back to the acquiring editor. Most publishers send the copyedited manuscript back to the author, and the right to see the manuscript at this stage is something worth fighting to have in your contract. Your job at this point is to go through the manuscript again and double-check the copy editor's revisions. Most of the time, these changes will have to do with grammar and consistency: this line of dialogue has a plural subject and a singular verb, or a double negative; on page 15, this character had blue eyes, but on page 45 and thereafter, her eyes are grey. Personally, I find this the most excruciating stage of any manuscript: even with the best copy editors I've ever had, the process is essentially one of having your nose rubbed in a succession of silly mistakes. This is a very unhelpful attitude— the copy editor is there to prevent your readers from pointing out the same silly mistakes—and one to be overcome if at all possible, but, to be honest, I'm still working on it. This is also the last chance to make any substantial changes to the manuscript, but big changes really shouldn't be necessary unless you've had to rush through one of the previous stages.

Once you've approved the copyedited manuscript, it moves to the publisher's production department. These are the people who are responsible for the overall look of the book—the typeface, decorative headers, design of the title page, cover art—and for actually getting the book to the printer. Generally, in science fiction publishing, the author has very little input at this stage of the process. Cover approval is rare except for the most important authors, and most of us are lucky to see a color photocopy of the artwork after it is approved by the editor. The first glimpse you're likely to get of the interior design is when the galleys are sent to you for proofreading. Galleys are the typesetter's first copy, and the publisher usually has them proofread by a professional; however, you should also go over them just in case the publisher's proofreader has a bad day. This is truly your last chance to make changes before the book goes to press, but be careful. Changes at this stage, except for the typesetter's errors, cost the publisher money that can in some cases be charged against your future earnings. Any significant revisions should have been made during the copyediting or earlier.

Then, finally, the manuscript goes to the printer. Copies are printed, bound, and shipped back to the publisher, who sends copies to bookstores, reviewers, and to you. In general, it takes about a year to go from the final draft of the manuscript to the actual book. It is possible to do it more quickly, but, except in the case of extremely timely books, it's not worth it to the publisher to make the extra effort. Your publisher will probably list your book in that month's ad in the SF magazines—trade magazines like *Locus* and the fiction magazines like *Analog*, *Asimov's*, and *Fantasy & Science Fiction*—and possibly in the program book of one or two conventions, but it is unlikely they'll do much more unless your book has the chance to become a major best-seller. You can do some self-promotion—appearances at local conventions, bookstores (especially the specialty stores), and so on—but by that point, you're probably working on your next book anyway. In any case, this is only a rough outline of the basic procedure you can expect. I'll be exploring more specific issues, problems, and potential solutions in the next chapter.

So far, I have presented the process as though you have to deal with publishers on your own, but of course you have a significant alternative: to find an agent to handle your work. I'll be considering the author/agent relationship in more detail in the next chapter, but in general the process of finding an agent is similar to that of finding a publisher. You research the various agencies, choose the one that seems most likely to meet your needs, and approach the agent about handling your work. Here a letter of inquiry is definitely the place to start, and you should enclose a SASE as well. If the agency is interested, a representative will ask you to send either three chapters and an outline, or the completed manuscript. After reviewing the matierals, an agent will let you know if he or she is interested in representing you. The advantage to having an agent is basically twofold: first, agents are likely to get you a faster reading at a publisher and, second, once an offer is made they are likely to get you better terms simply through familiarity with the norms of a publisher's contract. However, some publishers will still look at un-agented submissions, and you can learn to handle your own con-tracts if you're willing to make the effort. The disadvantage, of course, is that agents are paid by commission. That is, your agent will take 15 percent of the money you earn on deals that he or she brokered. Personally, I have always found 15 percent to be a rea-sonable fee for the services my agents have provided—but then, I've had good agents, and I don't have much tolerance for the necessary haggling that gets one a better contract.

However, whether you begin by looking for an agent or start out with blind submissions to a publisher, certain basic principles remain the same. First is the need to behave in the most profes-sional fashion possible. This is a variation on the old advice to job-hunters to dress as though they already had the position for which they had applied. While looking for your first agent or your first sale, you should behave as though you already had one—as though you were already a professional writer. I'm not advocating imitating those authors who throw public temper tantrums, or the ones you see holding forth at conventions either about how readers are too stupid to appreciate their brilliant work or, conversely, how they are only in this game for the money, not for anything so impractical as art or entertainment. The ones who do get away with this behavior (and there are fewer than you think) have to be twice as good as anyone else in order for publishers to put up with their antics, and they are not universally loved by their peers, or by those readers who have actually met them. (You may also notice that they are not as revered as they think they are—of course, given the size of the egos involved, it would be difficult for mere mortals to produce that level of adulation.) It does you no good to be noticed first as a loud-mouth, poseur, or, worst of all, nuisance. Despite most writers' secret dreams, the fact is that we are not rock stars: we do our enter-taining on the page, and most attempts to make ourselves look more interesting or important in person just make us look foolish and, worse, unprofessional.

There are some obvious *dos* and *don'ts* that you ignore at the very real risk of seeing a manuscript rejected, or having an agent decline to represent you. At the very least, ignoring these basic tenets means that even if you are accepted by the editor or agent, you are starting out with a question mark because you're falling below the professional standard.

First, *do* your research. Know roughly how your writing fits into the market, and know which publishers handle books like yours—there's no point in sending a cyberpunk novel to a publisher that handles primarily horror, or a horror novel to a house that specializes in hard SF. Even if an editor were to fall in love with your manuscript, she probably couldn't get it past the editorial committee, and if by some miracle she did, the marketing department would not be prepared to promote your novel effectively. If you're looking for an agent, ask yourself what you want from one. Do you want someone who can act as first editor, or do you have a writers' group that already performs that function? Are you interested in someone who can steer you to the latest opportunities and help you navigate the current trends? Or would you rather work with someone who wants authors to take their time building their own voice? Do you want the clout of a large agency, or the personal attention of a one-person shop? Find out what other writers a prospective agent represents: do they write in the same genre as you? If you're serious about writing science fiction, you want to be sure your agent is thoroughly familiar with those markets. What do other people think about this agent? Talk to current and former clients if possible.

If you get the chance to attend science fiction conventions, there are often panel discussions on getting published, or submitting a manuscript for the first time, on which editors, agents, and possibly a token author or two talk about how the business works. (A variation of this is the panel on which four or five first-time authors talk about how they got published.) This is free advice, and well worth attending. You will not only hear exactly what each editor is looking for, but also get a chance to see some of the personalities in the business. You may get a sense of who might be personally right for you. The same thing is true of lectures and discussions sponsored by other groups such as writers' consortia or universities: *do* take advantage of expert advice when you can get it.

But *don't* pay reader's fees. Despite attempts to work out an ethical way to handle these fees, the Association of Authors' Representatives (the group that represents agents) has decided that none of its members may charge them because of the potential for abuse, and you would be well advised to avoid anyone who tries.

Don't ignore the submission guidelines. Whether you're approaching an agent or a publisher, if they have stated the format that they want to see—query letter first, with SASE, manuscript to a particular person, and so on—give it to them. If you don't, nine times out of ten the manuscript will be returned to you unread.

In your query and cover letters, *do* be businesslike. It's to your advantage to be brief, to the point, and not to try too hard to sell yourself or the story. If you have previous sales, you should mention that, even if they are to small magazines or specialty presses; if someone has recommended you to that person, mention it—but don't overstate the case. If a writer who's otherwise a stranger to you mentioned that his agent is looking for the kind of story you're trying to sell, say precisely that—but don't claim undying friendship or a personal recommendation from that writer. Similarly, don't bother with personal information that isn't relevant to the novel you're trying to sell. If you're trying to sell a novel that hinges on chaos theory, it may be useful to the agent or editor to know that you're a professor of mathematics specializing in fractals. On the other hand, if you're trying to sell a horror novel about a demon birth, your academic credentials may be less important than the fact that you have borne two children. When in doubt, stick to business: tell the publisher or agent what the manuscript is about, and ask if they would like to see either three chapters and an outline, or the manuscript itself. And always enclose a SASE.

Do finish the manuscript first, before approaching anyone about selling it. The market is tight right now, and most editors (and therefore most agents) are unable to take a chance on an unknown author's ability to finish a novel. Many people can write three chapters, but then can't resolve the situation they've created. Even if you begin by sending three chapters and an outline, it's unlikely that you'll get an offer until the editor or agent has seen the finished manuscript; it's much more satisfying to you and to them if you have the full story waiting to send once they've decided they like the proposal.

If an agent or editor does request the full manuscript, *do* send it out in good condition, and in standard format. Editors and agents rely on their eyes to do their job. Anything less than a good clear copy is discourteous to them. *Don't* send in the manuscript with a page turned upside down somewhere in the second or third chapter. Some writers do this in the mistaken belief that they will then be able to tell if the editor or other reader actually reached that point because that person will turn the sheet rightside up again. This not only is ineffective (I know slush pile readers who delight in leaving the pages exactly as they found them) but also signals that you don't trust the publisher to give you a fair reading. That's no way to start a relationship.

Don't send out your only copy! (It shouldn't be necessary to say this, but it's better to take an extra day, pay the copy service, and make an extra copy of the manuscript instead of taking a chance on its being lost in the mail. The day you don't will be the day the local post office's sorting machine goes haywire and becomes a shredder.)

In your cover letters (and, for that matter, in your queries) *don't* try to justify or explain your manuscript. Nobody likes being told how they should feel about a story before they've had a chance to read it, but, more important, if your book is published, you won't have the chance to make those explanations to potential readers. The manuscript has to stand on its own.

Don't nag editors or agents. Your manuscript is not the only thing they're working on. Most editors have four or five projects on their desks at any one time (the really busy ones have twice that number), and agents represent dozens of clients. Expect the process to take time: many publishers' submissions guidelines also give you the average turn-around time. Don't follow up until that time has passed.

On the other hand, if you have to follow up, *do* nag effectively. An easy way to make sure a publisher has actually received your manuscript is to enclose a stamped, self-addressed postcard on which you've written something like, "Received _____ (date) by Major

Publishing House." Most editorial assistants (who are the people who open the manuscripts) will drop the postcard in the outbound mail. Even if they don't bother to date it, you'll have a postmark to let you know when it was sent. If, after three months or the stated turn-around time (whichever is longer), you still haven't heard anything, you can, and should, gently ask what's happening. A useful method is to send a letter with another stamped, self-addressed postcard asking the status of your manuscript. You could also e-mail the editor if you know the address, but not all editors like that method. Some receive more messages than they can comfortably handle, and others resent the fact that their company bears the cost of a response. (On the other hand, if the editors or agents express a preference for e-mail, believe them!) The telephone is probably the least effective way of checking on a manuscript. The chances of your interrupting an editor in the middle of something else important are fairly high, and no matter how polite you are, your telephone call is also a reminder of something that the editor hasn't yet done. Certainly you should never call just to see if someone has received your manuscript (that's what the postcard I mentioned earlier is for), and you shouldn't do anything until after the listed turn-around time has expired. The real risk you run is of making yourself enough of a nuisance that an editor will reject your manuscript just to be rid of you.

The same general principles apply to personal encounters with agents, editors, or other writers: *don't* harass them. Science fiction is a relatively small community of enthusiasts, and most writers, editors, and agents who specialize in it are also very much part of the community, participating in conventions, on-line discussions, and so on. It's very easy to meet them socially, even to become friendly with them, and the temptation to ask one of these nice people to read your manuscript can be overwhelming. Try to resist it, however. If you're dealing with editors or agents, remember that, by asking them to read your manuscript, or even to listen to you describe it to them, you have suddenly asked them to do their job. If the setting was a social one, you've suddenly changed the rules, and made this a business setting after all. The best way to handle such a situation is, first of all, not to put yourself or them into such an awkward position.

If you must, or if there are special circumstances—for example, after a panel discussion on which an editor encouraged first-time authors to submit manuscripts, or an agent admitted she was looking for clients—then keep it as businesslike as possible. Ask how you should go about making a submission, note down the answer, and go away, or at least end the business part of the conversation. Don't tell your new acquaintance what the book is about, or why you're their perfect author/client, unless they ask; in this case, actions, particularly professional ones, speak louder than words. The one exception to this would be a situation in which you have a manuscript that fits someone's particular, stated needs—if an editor is complaining that he can't seem to find any good novels on artificial life, for example, and you've just finished revising what you think is a brilliant version of the concept. In that case, you could mention that you have a manuscript completed that seems to be what they said they were looking for, and ask how you should go about submitting it. You want to keep things as polite and businesslike as possible, so that when you send in your manuscript or query letter mentioning this encounter, they will remember it with pleasure rather than with a wince of dismay.

The same principle applies to asking other writers to read and comment on your work, or to recommend it to their editors or agents. Most writers read very few manuscripts before publication, both for simple lack of time and because of the fear that they might be accused of plagiarism at some later date. (That's the reason that no writer I know ever reads an unsolicited manuscript, but returns it unopened.) In my experience, most people read only manuscripts from friends and colleagues with whom they have close working relationships, or manuscripts passed on to them by their agents, editors, or someone else whose professional judgment they trust. Remember, reading a manuscript is hard work: you're asking someone to take the time not only to read the story but to analyze what does and doesn't work, and to suggest possible solutions to any problems. If you find yourself in a situation where it seems appropriate to ask another writer if she or he would read your manuscript (and just meeting someone at a convention is not an appropriate situation), remember what you're asking, and don't be surprised or offended if that person begs off on the grounds of lack of time. If someone does agree to read your manuscript, expect criticism on a professional level—we all want every reader to love everything we do, but, realistically, you're much more likely to receive a mix of praise, criticism, and suggestion. You don't have to accept everything your readers say, but you did ask them to exercise their professional judgment. In the long run, their critical comments will probably do you as much good as their praise.

A corollary to this is this: *don't* demand explanations from editors who've rejected your work, or try to answer criticism from an outside reader. Editors reject most manuscripts with form letters, and they mean them: most manuscripts they get either don't meet their critical standards or are unsuited to their market. The former can be fixed, with work; the latter is something over which writers have no control. Even careful research can't always reveal that a particular house has just bought a novel very similar in premise to your alien-encounter novel, or that the new senior editor really doesn't like galaxy-spanning sagas. If you get a form rejection, file it if you must, but forget it and send the manuscript out again. Don't accost that editor at the next convention you both attend, demanding to know how she could have rejected your book with so little consideration, or, worse still, trying to explain why the editor's comments were worthless. You are not only unlikely to change the editor's mind, but you are also likely to put yourself on the mental list every editor has of people who are more trouble than they're worth. Besides, when your work does sell, and makes enormous amounts of money for you and your publisher, you want the rejecting editor to be kicking himself not just for failing to spot a best-seller, but for losing the chance to work with a consummate professional like yourself.

This is probably a good time to consider in more detail ways of coping with rejection. Every writer gets rejections; no matter how many sales you've made already, each rejection letter stings, a painful notice that you're not as good as you thought you were. Form rejection letters are bad enough, with their bland statement that "this manuscript does not meet our needs at this time" or a series of check boxes listing possible reasons for rejection. Still, you can always tell yourself that the editor had a bad day or that, if they were this stupid, clearly this wasn't the right publisher for you. A rejection letter that lays out reasons that you don't agree with is somewhat more painful: obviously, you didn't get through to the editor at all; he completely misunderstood your intent, and you're left with a prickly feeling of embarrassment. Still, you can console yourself with the thought that this wasn't the right house for you. Worst of all, however, is the rejection with comments that make clear that the editor understood exactly what you were trying to do, but didn't think you did it very well. Still, you can cope with any of these by calling a friend or fellow writer to complain, and then assuage the misery with a bottle of wine or a pint of Häagen-Dazs or Ben & Jerry's, depending on your preferred writerly stereotype, but these are mostly temporary measures. The usual advice is to send your manuscript back out again, and keep it circulating until it sells, and that probably is the best way to deal with a form rejection.

However, if you get specific comments, this is a good time to sit down and take a second look at your manuscript with those comments in mind. Try to feel good about getting feedback, even a negative response. Editors don't respond to every manuscript they see—they can't—and to have provoked one to write any comment, some explanation or suggestion or criticism, means that your manuscript got through to that editor in some way. Beyond that, however, this version of the manuscript didn't achieve its desired result, the sale, and the editor's comments may help you see why, and what changes, if any, you may want to make.

Comments like "It's a great idea, but you don't follow through" are often a way of saying that either the storytelling or the writing didn't succeed. If the problem is with your craft, then take a good hard look at what you've done. Use any specific comments as guidelines. Can you make changes that will address the editor's complaints? If the beginning is too slow, are you sure the important events of your story start to happen in the first chapter? If your first few chapters are all background, then consider presenting that information in flashbacks, and start the manuscript at the point at which things start to happen. If you must have a long period of stage-setting, try thinking of things that could happen to keep the readers' interest while you inform them. If you don't agree with the specific comments—if, for example, the editor rejected your manuscript because your carefully worked out future slang was too confusing, and that speech pattern is absolutely crucial to the story you want to tell—then is there a way you can address the problem without following the editor's specific suggestions? Can you make the dialogue clearer without dropping the slang, or can you clarify it through the narrative? Editors are generally very good at identifying problems; they're more fallible, however, when it comes to providing solutions. Besides, the writing is *your* job.

Criticisms based on misunderstanding what you were trying to say are a little harder to handle. The first step is probably to try to figure out how an otherwise perceptive reader (this editor had to be perceptive or you wouldn't have sent it to her, right?) got it so very wrong. In a very few cases, you may not be able to find anything except the suspicion that you pushed this editor's buttons, or that the manuscript arrived on a very bad day. If you really can't find anything, chalk it up to experience, and treat it like a form rejection: send the manuscript somewhere else. In other cases, you may suddenly realize that you left out some crucial bit of information, and without it the editor had no other way to read the manuscript. It's embarrassing, but at least you know how to fix the problem. Most often, though, it will be a combination of the editor's preferences and the author's lack of clarity. Then you need to spend some time with the manuscript and figure out, if you can, why the editor felt that way. If the problem is your protagonist, can you see from the comments why the editor didn't or couldn't identify with the character? The protagonist may not have had enough shadings to seem interesting, or have seemed pallid in comparison with a secondary character; or you may have spent too much time on unimportant details of the character's life at the expense of the story. Your character may have been too passive, reacting to events rather than acting on his or her own initiative. If your character isn't part of the contemporary mainstream, maybe this editor couldn't find a way into the character's reality; you can look either for a way to make the character more accessible without compromising your story, or for a more responsive editor. If it's the story—an ending that an editor finds "unsatisfying," for example—the same options are available.

You should take a hard look at the problem that the editor has identified—why the ending might not satisfy expectation—and then decide if you want to make changes, or if the break with expectation is important enough to the story you want to tell that you have to keep it intact.

Rejection that comes from understanding what you wanted to say and either thinking you didn't do it well enough or that it wasn't worth doing is actually a little easier to handle. If an editor gives you comments that convince you that he understood what you were reaching for, but thinks that you missed it, you have to take those comments very seriously. After all, you succeeded in communicating your goal; the editor's job is to point out the missteps along the way, and you should take advantage of his expertise. Give yourself time to get over the emotional reaction, and take a hard look at the comments and your manuscript. Are the problems with the writing itself, the story-telling, the characters, or even the science? Are these problems that can be fixed, or would you be better off putting this manuscript aside for a while, and concentrating on a new project?

Dealing with someone who not only understands what you wanted to do but rejects your whole intent is a tricky problem, the sort of thing you run into when you try to push the envelope, either personally or in terms of the genre. I once had an agent reject a story of mine not so much because it was badly done but because "the only difference between this manuscript and a dozen others novels is that the main characters are women." That was the point, and I felt that it was important to tell this story with women at the center; however, I wasn't able to convince this agent of that, and I have never sold the novel. In this case, the novel was rejected because the story as I presented it wasn't considered to be important enough. If that should happen to you, I'd encourage you to stick to your story, at least in principle. You might look for a way to make it more accessible to readers who aren't familiar with the point of view you're taking, but not at the cost of losing the story you wanted to tell. Can you narrow the focus of your story, so that the reasons you think it's important become starkly clear? Can you broaden the focus, so that the story's importance is placed in a fuller context? Is it worth your while to put the project on hold, and come back to it when you've built a following or improved your writing skills to the point where the manuscript will be too good to refuse? Should you just shrug off the criticism and approach a different publisher? Each situation will be different, but my main advice is not to give up on your goals. I've addressed previously the importance of passion: never let someone talk you out of writing a story that is vitally important to you.

The best way to deal with a rejection that includes comments is probably to treat it like any other criticism. There's a kind of paradox involved: on the one hand, you need to have the self-confidence to reject inappropriate comments and suggestions, and on the other, you need to have the humility (and realistic outlook) to consider every critical comment as a possible indicator of something you can improve. (I've heard this described in shorthand as, "Believe every-thing everybody tells you, but don't accept anything anybody tells you.") Most people can tell you when something doesn't work in a story, but only a few can tell you precisely what it is. (Being able to articulate problems is what editors are paid to do.) Ideally, you'll be able to make changes in a way that answers their questions but pre-serves your original intent.

It may seem a little odd to talk about coping with sales, but a sale can be almost as unnerving as a rejection. For one thing, selling a novel means that you're suddenly catapulted into an entirely differ-ent world: you're officially a professional now, and you have to deal with the business side of the job in a way you never had to before. Even getting an agent means that you have to handle your writing differently, producing material more regularly and getting it to your agent so that he or she can get it to the publishers. A contract means both money coming in and deadlines you have to meet. Getting paid means paying taxes, and neither your publisher nor your agent will withhold them for you. Speaking as someone who made this mistake early in her career, it's a very good idea to start putting away a little bit of money to cover the tax bill—and remem-ber, it's federal tax, state tax (if any), *and* self-employment tax. In my case, I was a graduate student when I sold my first novel, and had almost no other income and therefore no withheld taxes to offset what I owed. You're better off saving more than you need than getting a nasty shock in April! If there are significant revisions to be made, or even minor ones, make sure you can make them in time to the meet the contract's delivery date. You don't want to be late with your first novel.

Finally, be realistic about what a first sale means. This is the first step toward a career, not the career itself. Don't expect your publisher to commit large amounts of time and money toward publicity. Science fiction publishers don't spend a lot of money on advertising outside the specialty magazines, and they almost never spend a lot of money on a first novel. You can do a certain amount through judicious self-promotion—by going to science fiction conventions and appearing on panels, by arranging solo or group signings at local bookstores, and so on—and you can use some of your author's copies to try to get the book reviewed by sources other than the usual genre outlets. (However, be realistic: you're more likely to get a response from your alumni magazine, a professional journal covering the subject of your novel, and your local newspaper than you are from the *New York Times*, and besides, your publisher will probably send the book to the *Times* if she thinks there's any chance it could be reviewed there.) If your agent or editor makes promotional suggestions, follow them if you possibly can. The main thing you need to do is to start working on the next book: there's enough that can go wrong without dooming yourself to become the literary equivalent of a one-hit wonder.

12

CHAPTER

Agents and Publishers

IT MAY SEEM RATHER ODD TO LUMP TWO SUCH ADVERSARIAL groups into a single chapter, but your relationships with them will be surprisingly similar. Both exist to help you make your work the best it can be; both can hurt you if you're not clear about what you want and about what each one can, and can't, do for you. You can save yourself a lot of grief later on by understanding what you can reasonably expect from each one of them.

Agents exist to help authors sell their manuscripts. They make their living by taking a commission (usually 15 percent, though some still charge 10 percent) on each sale, so their incentive to makes sales is naturally high. How do agents help sell your manuscript, and, beyond that, what can you expect your agent to do for you? As explained in the last chapter, there are two basic reasons to use an agent. The first is access: agents are closely attuned to the markets, to the internal politics of the major publishers, and to the individual editors' likes and dislikes. When agents take on a manuscript, they usually have some idea of where they will start trying to sell it, and which other publishers and editors would be possible markets. More than that, however, an agent's submission promises an editor that the manuscript already meets basic professional standards, and that the agent, who is also a professional reader of science fiction, thinks the story has sufficient merit to make it publishable. A manuscript submitted blind, without an agent's representation, goes directly to the slush pile, and languishes there until the harried first reader gets around to it; the same manuscript, submitted by an agent, goes directly to the editor's desk. Both manuscripts may be bought or rejected, but the process takes longer without an agent's help.

The second reason to have an agent is to get better deals. It's an agent's job to know about publisher's contracts, all the minutiae of subrights and subclauses, and to know which provisions each publisher considers negotiable and which are inviolable. More basically, it's an agent's job to know both what the standard advance should be, and whether or not you'll be hurt by asking for more. By that, I don't just mean whether or not asking for more money will break the deal, though of course that's part of it. I also mean whether in the long term it's better to take a slightly smaller advance that will produce a more realistic print run—the number of copies printed—and overall better sales, or whether a publisher that generally offers smaller advances but supports its backlist (books published earlier) is better for your book than one that offers larger advances but only intermittent support.

A final reason to have an agent is to insulate yourself from the process of negotiation. If you are responsible for haggling over the details of the contract—a process that often raises tempers or at least frays one's tolerance for the other party—once it's signed, you then have to turn around and work closely and cooperatively with the same person who has been your adversary throughout the contract negotiations. Some people find this easy, but if you don't, using your agent as a buffer can preserve good relations with your editor.

Personally, I've always used an agent, primarily because I dislike negotiating. To me, it is well worth 15 percent to have someone else handle the details of the contracts and the haggling that goes into getting the best possible deal. This doesn't mean I can ignore what my agent does (well, actually I could, at least in terms of trust, but I prefer to be more involved than that), but the things I don't like are divorced from direct contact with the editor with whom I'll be working for the next eight to twelve months. My agent and I discuss what I want from a contract before he begins negotiations, and then he refers major decisions to me. I listen carefully to his advice and generally follow it, or have a good reason for doing something else.

The process of finding an agent has been discussed at such length in so many other books and magazines that I'm going to touch on it only briefly here. (For an extremely helpful handling of the process, I recommend Donald Maass's *The Career Novelist*. Maass is himself an agent, and covers your likely choices and options in great detail.) Probably the most important part of the process, however, is the one that doesn't get discussed as much as it should. You need to ask yourself what you want from an agent. That may seem kind of odd—all agents do basically the same thing, right?—but matching your short- and long-term goals with an agent who is good at achieving them is probably the single factor that will create and maintain a good relationship with an agent. Ask yourself what kind of novels you write. Are they exciting adventures, or carefully crafted extrapolation, or experimental prose? Is this book the first of a projected series or trilogy, or a stand-alone novel? Where do you want to be in a year? In five years? Once you know what you want to do, you can ask your potential agent the same kinds of questions—where does he or she see your career going? Is he or she sympathetic to your goals, and to your ambitions for your books? You should ask as well business questions like the amount of the commission, the agency size, what happens to your money if the agent dies or is incapacitated for any length of time, and so forth.

After you've sorted out what you're looking for, the process of finding an agent is similar to that of finding a publisher. You begin with research, collecting names and information about the agency. Factors to consider are the size of the agency, its location (it's not absolutely necessary that an agent be located in New York, but there are times when being in the same time zone as you or your publisher can be a factor!), and whether the agent or agency is used to handling the kind of books you write. At the very least, if you intend to go on writing science fiction, you should look for an agent who is familiar with the field and its publishers and editors. You should also check out their other credentials, such as membership in the Association of Authors' Representatives, and their reputation among established pros. Once you've picked a likely agency, send a query letter, telling them you're looking for an agent. Give a brief description of the novel you're ready to sell (you do have one finished, right?), and ask if they'd like to see three chapters and an outline, or the completed manuscript. And then you wait.

Once an agent does accept you, however, it's a good idea to go back over your original list of criteria to make sure this person will meet your needs. Talk to your agent about your plans, and see if she thinks they're realistic, and if she seems willing to work with your framework. If she's not, listen to what she suggests: it may make sense for you to change your mind (if you've been overambitious, or underambitious, for that matter), or it may make sense for you to thank her for her time and look elsewhere. Above all, ask yourself if this is a person you could stand to work with for the next five, seven, or ten years. If not, you may want to look elsewhere. You are probably better off without an agent than making yourself unhappy by trying to work with the wrong one.

One other thing to consider in looking at agents is their editorial style. Not many years ago, agents sold manuscripts to editors who then edited them. These days, however, as publishers are increasingly merged into massive conglomerates used to high profit margins, fewer and fewer editors are able to take a chance on a manuscript that is not essentially publishable as they first see it. No longer are they able to buy a manuscript that has promise but needs a major rewrite, and then talk the author through that process of revision. Instead, that job increasingly falls to your agent. A manuscript that still needs work is likely to land on your agent's desk, and to come back to you with his or her comments and suggestions for revision before it ever reaches a publisher. If your agent's editorial interests match your needs, your job will be made that much easier.

Once you have an agent you like, who is enthusiastic about your work and whose style and attitude are compatible with your own, you should take some pains to keep the relationship going. Bear in mind what is, and isn't, reasonable to expect from him—and remember, if nothing else, you're not your agent's only client. There will be times when you can't get through as quickly as you'd like, or when his attention is diverted to someone else's career. This happens to everyone sometimes; it's only when that's the normal tone of your relationship that you should consider going elsewhere. Your agent is not your therapist; however, he is the one person with whom you can afford to be completely open about your career. Part of the agent's job is to act as a buffer between you and the rest of the professional world, so he is the person to approach with tricky professional questions—how to answer an importunate fan letter, whether a copy editor went too far, how to deal with an important editor whom you personally dislike, even how best to apologize for getting sick at a publisher's party and vomiting on someone's shoes. Your agent is also the person to go to if you have problems with your writing. He needs to know if a manuscript is going to be delayed so that he can arrange things with your editor, and he may also be able to suggest ways of resolving your problem, working through a block, or even extending the contract.

You should also keep your agent informed of any publicity you do. If you run off flyers for your latest novel to be distributed at a local convention, send a copy to your agent, too. If you're doing a bookstore signing, either alone or with other authors, let your agent know. The same goes for lectures or speeches: keep your agent informed. Each of these activities is something she can use to promote you later. If your book is reviewed or if you're interviewed in a local paper or magazine, make sure you get a copy for your agent as well as for yourself. Agents see most of the big literary outlets, but nobody can keep track of all the smaller sources. If you get an interview in the local underground paper (one of the better experiences of my career, actually), or in a specialty source outside the SF field, you can be pretty sure your agent won't see it unless you send her a copy. The more clippings and reviews your agent has, the better prepared she, and you, will be for the day you suddenly need a press release celebrating a major sale.

Finally, if you have a good agent, let people know. Thank your agent for doing a good job, and if other writers ask you about him or her, tell them honestly what you think. No one will think less of you if you give credit to your agent for making a good deal, or more of you for hogging the credit. On the other hand, if you find that your relationship with your agent isn't working any more, it's all right to move on to someone else. It's even possible to do it and remain on good terms. My first agent was excellent at handling new authors, at selling the first two to five novels. However, he was less good at building careers beyond that point, and at the same time my goals had changed from what they had been when I joined his agency. The fact that my publisher and I were on the east coast, while my agent was on the west coast—the time changes usually added twenty-four hours to any decision—exacerbated the situation, and I decided to look for, and found, a new agent. I was honest with my old agent about my reasons for moving on, and with my new agent about why I'd come to him, and as a result I not only am happy with my current agent, but also remain on good terms with my former agent. This is important, because the agent who sells a manuscript generally continues to handle everything arising from that contract. If you leave on bad terms, and have several books still in print being handled by that agent, it becomes even harder to arrange further sales or even to handle royalties.

Obviously, your relationship with your editor will be different from that with your agent. On the most fundamental level, your agent is primarily concerned with you and your overall career, while your editor is primarily concerned with each book as it appears. What your editor wants from you is a manuscript that will sell well enough to justify its existence; most editors also want the best possible manuscript you can provide. Most editors buy books only if they believe they fit both criteria. In the old days (which were still going strong as recently as six or seven years ago), editors were able to buy books that weren't quite ready to be published, and work with authors until the stories were burnished to near perfection. While current market conditions and mergers in the publishing industry have made this situation uncommon to the point of nonexistence, editors still want to edit. They want to help you make your manuscript better, and to that end the good ones offer not only analysis of your story but genuinely helpful suggestions.

As you move on in your career, however, it becomes more likely that you will start selling novels on a proposal rather than on a completed manuscript, and at this stage your relationship with your editors becomes crucial. When editors buy a book from a proposal, they are really buying a plot summary based on the promise of your previous books. Although they've committed the publisher to the manuscript, the draft that arrives on their desks is always something of a surprise to them, no matter how closely you followed your proposal. Revisions, or at least requests for them, are almost inevitable.

This is not a bad thing: editors ask you to revise in order to make your book better, not just more salable, but genuinely a better piece of work. As always when people make suggestions, believe every-thing and none of it. Pay particular attention to the problems an editor sees: those are likely to be real, even if you don't want to make the specific changes that have been requested. You can usu-ally find another way to resolve the question that's been raised. If you think the revisions are a good idea, but are going to take extra time—more than a couple of weeks, say—let the editor know that as soon as you know. If you have an agent, tell your agent and let him or her deal with it, but your editor needs to know if there is going to be a significant delay. Give your editor realistic answers to deadline questions: most editors would rather know now that your manuscript is going to be four months late than to be fobbed off with eight repetitions of "just another two weeks."

Some editors like to see work in progress; others prefer not to deal with anything less then a completed manuscript. Writers are just as personal in their preferences. I hate to show unfinished work to anybody except a pair of fellow writers who are also close friends—and that pair doesn't include my editor. This isn't a matter of trust; I simply want my editor to see the finished, fully revised manuscript with fresh eyes, unclouded by any memory of previous drafts. Other writers like to send in a partial manuscript or an early complete draft for comment before moving on to the final draft. This is a matter for you and your editor to work out between yourselves, but not every editor will have the time to look at early drafts.

However, there are a few situations that you should discuss with your editor before committing yourself to them. The obvious one is any major departure from the proposal. Your editor bought the book in the proposal; if you're going to change that significantly, you need to tell him as soon as possible. He may well agree that this new idea is much better, a brilliant departure, but he also needs time to prepare the marketing department and everyone else con-cerned for the changes. Another case in which your editor's early input is probably advisable is if you're planning a major change in tone or style—if you're going from hard SF to light comedy, or from social satire to grueling adventure, or if you're leaving one successful series to do something different. In this case, the editor knows you're making a big change, and will want to help you do it well; talk to him throughout the writing process, and set up early or partial delivery dates if you both think that would be helpful.

Your acquiring editor is not the only person you will deal with at your publisher. Inevitably, you will confront the copy editor, usually a nameless, faceless person whom you will know only through the penciled comments on your returned manuscript. As I've said before, the copy editor's job is to read a finished manuscript before it goes into production, looking for errors in consistency and anything that isn't completely clear. Good copy editors are worth their weight in rubies: these are the people who catch the spelling errors you and your computer missed, who remember on page 303 that you already used that character's name back on page 58, who gently point out that the equation you cite is actually called Sullivan's Law, and it's not related to chaos theory—and provide you with the name you really meant to use. A good copyediting job may leave you a little embarrassed ("I can't *believe* I missed that!"), but well aware of the potentially much larger humiliation it's saved you. A really good copy editor has an ear for the rhythm of your prose, and works with it to preserve your style even while clearing up any unintended confusion. Unfortunately, with the increasing number of junior editors who are also copy editors, the line between copy editing and real editing is increasing blurred. It is not the copy editor's job to rewrite your prose, except for things like suggesting a synonym for a too-often repeated word. It's not a copy editor's job to suggest substantive revisions, or any revisions that aren't intended to improve clarity. When a copy editor does this, you have the right to ignore their suggestions (or to accept them, of course), and to insist that your original phrasing be put back. If you decide to ignore them, you should also let your editor know what you're doing. Use your common sense in handling an intrusive copy edit, and if you're really angry, try to get an unbiased eye to check over the manuscript and make sure you're not overreacting. In general, though, the copy editor is likely to be right about grammar and whether or not you've used the term differently before.

The other major issue between writers and publishers tends to be the matter of cover art. Everyone has heard horror stories about inappropriate and inaccurate covers—my personal favorite (I own this one) is an edition of Samuel R. Delany's *Babel-17* that depicts the protagonist, a small, slight Asian poet named Rydra Wong, as an Amazonian blonde in a metal bikini. Silence Leigh, the protagonist of my own *Five-Twelfths of Heaven*, shows up in the cover art as a blonde, despite being described in the text as dark-haired. On the other hand, publishers complain quite legitimately that authors have no idea about what makes a good cover—one that catches readers' eyes and induces them to buy the book. I've been generally happy with my covers at my current publisher, Tor Books; the best ones, which are very good indeed, have been done by the same artist, Nicholas Jainschigg, and have been given a unifying style that helps readers recognize that this is another novel by Melissa Scott. The cover for *Trouble and Her Friends* was instrumental in getting that book noticed by bookstores and reviewers; the art for *Night Sky Mine* (which was done even before Nick had read the manuscript) perfectly captures the way I imagined the protagonist should look. The only catch to all of this is that I had absolutely nothing to do with any of it: with the exception of a very few, very important writers, science fiction writers generally have no input at all into the overall design of the book. Often an editor will send you a cover flat—the proof copy, if you will—but that's a courtesy rather than an author's right. If you can persuade your editor to do this for you, take advantage of it. This is the only chance you'll have to spot serious mistakes—like misspelled names, or missing initials, as happened to my coauthor on *Point of Hopes*—that would otherwise appear in the final printing.

Is there anything you can do to protect yourself against a misleading cover? Not a great deal, I'm afraid, particularly early on in your career. If your editor is willing to discuss the matter, and not all of them are, you can offer a few cautious suggestions. If you do get the chance, don't try to dictate the cover art ("I want the cover to show the scene where . . ."). Instead, your best bet is to talk about what you see as the book's main market, and why you think a particular strategy might work well, or should be avoided. ("I'm really concerned about making sure readers know they're picking up an experimental novel, not a standard hard SF narrative; is there some way that the cover can signal that, so that it reaches the right people, and doesn't disappoint anyone?") You may—you probably will—be ignored, but if you can demonstrate a solid marketing point, you may have a chance of getting through on the next book. For example, my books should logically do well in women's bookstores: they generally feature strong women as protagonists, and most of them have an explicitly feminist worldview. However, until *Trouble and Her Friends*, I was not well represented in those stores. The problem, according to several women's bookstore owners, was the cover art, which featured either no people or primarily men. Their readers, reasonably or not, wanted books with women on the cover, a visual promise that women were at the center of these stories. I was able to pass that on to my editor at Tor; whether or not my comment had results, the last two novels I've done with female protagonists have featured those characters on the covers.

Finally, in dealing with your agent and editor, be professional. Be aware of and respect the other demands on their time—you aren't anybody's sole author—and minimize the amount of trivia that you place on their desks. When you need a sizable block of either one's time, arrange it in advance, and then be prompt for the appointment. If someone tells you not to expect to hear from her for a month, believe her. Then give her an extra week before calling to see what's going on. Be straightforward—particularly with your agent—and ask your agent and editor to be straightforward with you. If you can possibly manage it, keep your emotions out of the relationship—or at least wait until you've calmed down before calling your editor about the latest copy editing horror or dreadful cover art. There will come a day when your only possible response to something is to be screamingly angry. If you have always before been perfectly polite, reasonable, and willing to compromise, your anger will be that much more effective. Remember that there is a difference between friendship and business. It's hard doing business with your friends, and the relationships between an author and agent, and an author and an editor, are business relationships first of all. The artistic relationship comes second, unfortunately, but friendship needn't be a part of the equation. When it is, it's wonderful—I once sold a short story to a close friend, and got some of the most perceptive and rigorous editing I've ever had—but it's not necessary. All that you really need is mutual respect and courtesy. If you're not getting that, it's time to leave.

13

CHAPTER

Moving On

WITH A LITTLE LUCK AND SOME JUDICIOUS PLANNING, YOUR first sale will be only the beginning of your career. You'll move from writing on spec to selling from proposals, from being a weekend writer to quitting the day job and writing full time, from paperback original to hardcover, and maybe even to best-seller status. As you build your career, however, there are some things that you can do to make the process easier. If writing is your desired career, then you have to pay attention to the business and professional sides of it as well as to the writing itself. Although nothing you do will destroy really good writing, or make up for really bad writing, there are plenty of things you can do to make your life a little easier.

The first, and probably the most basic thing you can do, is to make an effort to learn the ropes. Make sure you discuss the reasons for your agent's choices as well as your various options; if he has the time, ask him to discuss strategy in a broad sense as well as in the ways it personally applies to you. (This can be very helpful when you're confronted with a peer who has suddenly made an enormous leap in advance money or number of books being printed. Talking to your agent may help you feel better—your agent may offer you some sound reasons for not taking that step at this particular point in your career.) Read books on writing that deal with the business side as well as the creative side, and consider subscribing to writers' magazines that do the same. Don't rush right out and do each thing the books and articles suggest, however. Instead, use them as a knowledge base, and stay aware of the reasons each writer gives for doing something. Listen to your fellow writers: if they've all had a bad experience with a certain publisher, you should probably think twice before submitting your book there. The Science Fiction and Fantasy Writers of America can offer resources as well, though all too often the useful information is drowned in a flood of generic complaints and politics. However, the SFFWA *Handbook*, published by Writer's Notebook Press in 1990, contains a number of helpful essays. Be aware of the markets and of the other books that are being published. *Locus* is considered to be the trade magazine of the genre, and is still the most complete resource of its kind. You don't want to be ruled by the markets, but it's good to know the kinds of books that are selling, the publishers who are buying, and the general levels of advances and royalties. If you don't have an agent, that kind of information is ten times more important to you; even if you do have one, keeping abreast of the field makes both your jobs easier.

Two options that you are likely to encounter as you move on in your career are packaged deals and work-for-hire. Although the distinction between the two is a little blurry—most packagers are offering essentially work-for-hire—the bottom line is pretty similar. In both cases, you the writer are producing a work whose copyright belongs by contract to someone else. You don't have any rights in it, except those specified by contract; once it's off your desk, it belongs to the person who commissioned it, and your stake in it has ended. The main difference between the two is that a packager buys a book from you and then turns around and sells it to a publisher, while straight work-for-hire is commissioned directly by the publisher. Why would anyone do this kind of writing? The money tends to be very good: I have received larger advances for paperback Star Trek novels than I have for my own original fiction, published in hardback. Also, generally, the work is a lot less. It took me about eight to twelve weeks to complete the Star Trek novels, including the time spent writing the proposal—as compared to eight to twelve months to write one of my own novels. The latter doesn't include the one or two years of research and preparation, either. Another reason that many beginning writers give is that, in effect, doing a media tie-in novel or a volume in a packaged series lets them learn to write on the job.

There is a certain truth to all these rationales, but there are enough potential pitfalls to make work-for-hire or any packaged deal something to approach with caution. Money is always a temptation to any writer—advances tend to be smaller than we'd like, and are often paid in installments, half on signing the contract and half on the delivery of the completed manuscript, so that one advance actually provides two years' income. And the numbers on packages or work-for-hire are usually really good. However, the basic problem with packaged deals should be fairly obvious. A packager functions by paying you the writer a fixed sum for a completed manuscript, and then turning around and selling that manuscript (and others in the series) to a publisher. The packager's profit comes from paying you as little as possible, and getting as much as possible from the publisher. From the packager's point of view, this is perfectly reasonable: after all, the packager did all the work of thinking up the idea, and maybe even creating the basic characters and plots, and then sold the package to a publisher. All the writers do is produce actual manuscripts, for which they are appropriately compensated. But when the package is being sold for $100,000 a novel, and you are getting only $50,000 for the novel or novels you wrote (and half of the fee would be a pretty generous arrangement), it's hard not to wonder what the packager did that was worth half the pay for your work, particularly when a standard agency agreement on the same book would net you $85,000, less your agent's expenses.

The fundamental difference between an agent and a packager is that the more money you make, the more money your agent makes. The more money you make in a packaged deal, the less money the packager makes. Who's more likely to work harder for your interests? On the other hand, sometimes having the money right now is more important than any future profits, and in that case doing a packaged novel may suit your needs. I would recommend, however, that you make sure you are paid for any work you do, like outlines, treatments, or proposals, before you do it, and that your contract is explicit about your rights, if any, in the manuscript you produce. Most of all, don't let yourself be tied to a package in order to get yourself published. A multiple-book deal, particularly if the package is a success, just sets you up for arguments over money.

Media (or game) tie-ins function a lot like packaged books, but the publisher is its own packager. With these books, the publisher has generally bought the rights to commission novels featuring licensed characters or situations, and the manuscripts must be approved not only by the publisher but by the owner of the original source as well. As with a packaged deal, the publisher or the owner of the original material retains most if not all rights in the completed manuscript, and pays nothing or a purely nominal royalty against the (usually large) advance. The publisher and owner have usually worked out very strict guidelines that cover the kinds of stories they want to see, how the characters are to be presented, and sometimes the overall tone of the novels. In a novel based on series television, for example, the novel is expected to be structured like an episode of the show, and, again like a series, is expected to return the characters to the same (neutral) emotional state they occupied at the beginning of the story. Because your novel seeks to recreate the experience readers have when they watch the show or play the game, you had better enjoy and appreciate the original material. If you don't, you will not only have a miserable time writing it, but also are likely to miss some of the crucial emotional triggers, and be forced to spend more time rewriting before you get it right.

The other arguments for doing this kind of work are generally that any writing will teach you to write better, and that any publication is better than no publication when it comes time to sell your own original work. Frankly, I don't think either of these holds up to closer scrutiny. Writing a packaged series novel or a media tie-in novel teaches you how to write only from someone else's idea—and to write to a strict and not very imaginative format, at that. What it can't teach you is how to create a world and characters from scratch, or how to catch and hold your readers' interest through the course of a novel. Publishers know this, and will treat your first original novel after a dozen media tie-ins as exactly what it is: a first novel by an unknown quantity. There's also no guarantee that you'll take readers with you from the series or the tie-ins to your own work:

most of the people who read these novels regularly know what they like, and what they like is the books they've already read.

On the other hand, if you've already published a few novels, and you can stand the loss of high literary status that can come with publishing in this area, the money is good. If you enjoy the original source, you might find yourself being paid very well for something that was good, undemanding fun. Make sure you understand all the ramifications of your contract, including who owns what rights and whether the publisher can have someone else rewrite your work without taking your name off it, and make sure you fully understand the limits and structure of the series. (Most editors who handle this kind of book are thorough, if cynical, in their explanations.) Finally, make sure that you budget enough time to do the job right, so that you can use that big advance to support your original work.

Publicity is another issue that you will confront early in your career. I've never met anyone who didn't think their publisher could be getting more publicity for them—that just a little more advertising or a better placement in the bookstores would sell thousands of extra copies. At the same time, I've met very few writers who even try to arrange for any of that on their own. Some of the ones who do push far too hard though, and end up spending more time on embarrassing publicity stunts than they do on their writing. However, you don't have either to spend your money or to force yourself to do anything that's uncongenial to you to get some extra attention for your books.

The simplest thing to try is to arrange a signing or a reading at your local bookstore, preferably to be held right around the time that your book comes out. (This is one of the reasons to stay on good terms with your local bookstore: the more they like you, the more willing they're likely to be to host an event like this.) If you've ever been to a bookstore during such an event, however, you've probably experienced the situation that every author dreads: one lone writer perched at a table behind a stack of books, while everyone in the store (except perhaps his mother) tries to ignore his presence. There are a few things you can do to avoid this. First, try to get a time when you can bully most of your friends into showing up for part of the event. The more bodies you bring in, the better it is for you and for the store. Second, try to have the signing a little bit before the book is available in other stores. Bookstores can usually get copies shipped to them a little early for a special event, and if you have any following at all, you can hope they'll show up to get an early copy. Third, do some of the publicity yourself. The bookstore will usually put up posters in its windows, and may notify your local paper's arts calendar, but ask when you arrange the signing. If they don't arrange for listings, you can do it—the guidelines and the deadline for submission are usually printed in the paper, or you can get them direct from your newspaper. If you maintain a Web site for your writing, put up a notice; if you frequent on-line discussion groups or participate in mailing lists where such an announcement would be appropriate, by all means, let people know what's happening. (On Genie, for example, the writers' topics often carry notices of signings or readings, and at least one of the system operators was particularly good about copying the information to other relevant topics.) You might even spend a little money, and send out postcards to all your friends and relatives who might possibly attend. The main thing is to get people there.

Another way to draw bodies into a signing is to join forces with several other writers—three is a good number, more than five gets awkward—and hope that each of you brings a few readers. You should do the same kinds of personal publicity—get the event listed, inform your friends, and so on—and encourage the other writers to do the same.

Readings are a little more complicated than signings, both because of the awkward space available in most bookstores, and because you're offering something more than your mere presence. However, readings, particularly with several authors participating, can draw more of a crowd than a signing, so they're often worth the extra effort. Make sure you know how much time you have, and that the piece you intend to read will fit into the allotted space. If you're reading from a novel, figure out what you need to say by way of introduction and background information, and then time that, too, so that your full presentation fits into the time you've been given. If your reading takes every one of the twenty minutes you were given, and then your introduction takes five more, at best you're running overtime, and at worst you've taken that five minutes from the other people on the program. Not everyone reads aloud well: if you're not one of the naturals, practice before you do it in public. Even if you do read well, rehearse a few times. You're bound to find some lines that could use extra emphasis, that, with just the right inflection, will give you a laugh or produce a frisson of excitement. Some people's prose was written to be seen as much as heard, and if you fall into that category, as I do, you'll need to edit some of the stage directions and descriptions (and, in my case, the complex sentence structures) for verbal presentation. If your voice is weak, either make sure you're working in a small enough space that you can be heard, or arrange—in advance—to have a microphone set up for you. Sometimes the sound system is bad enough to do you more harm than good. If this happens to you (it's happened to me), don't be afraid to ask people to move down front and abandon the mike. Make sure you have a glass of water handy, just in case. If you can, relax and enjoy yourself. The people who've come to hear you read want to like you. They want to enjoy your work, and they'll meet you halfway if you give them the chance.

If there are science fiction specialty stores in your area, they are the natural people to approach about either signings or readings. Their customers are your most likely readers, and both specialty bookstore owners and readers are always looking for new material. Independent bookstores are your next best choice. They're able to make decisions for themselves, and are often very supportive of local talent. The owners are usually the managers, and are in business for the long run, so you can establish a long-term relationship with that store. The large chains have less autonomy, and are rarely laid out in a way that facilitates events. Some may host only major authors' tours, while others may not do any promotional events outside those mandated by the chain. Some may be delighted to have you, and throw a lovely party, complete with wine and cheese, that sells multiple copies of your book—and then turn you down next year because the manager has moved on or the chain's policy has changed.

It is also possible, particularly as your career builds, to convince local (and not so local) newspapers and magazines to interview you, and possibly to review your books. Certainly if you win awards, you should send a press release to your local newspaper(s)—some awards committees will do this for you, but there's no harm in sending one yourself. You should also send press releases announcing the publication of your latest book. Even if nothing happens directly, the editor of the arts section may remember your name when she has a gap to fill. Keep an eye out, too, for other possibilities. My local newspaper has a daily "Bright" (the editor took seriously a complaint that he published only bad news) and at least one fellow novelist has gotten his awards publicized through that feature. If you're serious about self-promotion, you should stay alert to similar possibilities. It's also worth your while to give some thought to areas that your publisher probably won't cover, or can't cover as effectively as you can. If your book might appeal to readers outside the science fiction mainstream, you might try to think of ways to reach them as well. I mentioned earlier my attempts to get my novels into women's bookstores (and the unexpected problem I encountered); I've also been able to get my books reviewed in some gay and lesbian magazines that don't ordinarily cover science fiction because the books feature gay and lesbian characters. This is not something my publisher is prepared to do—it's not that they were unwilling to send copies, but they didn't know whom to contact, or where to send the review copies. If your books might similarly appeal to an outside audience, the connection may be worth pursuing. You have nothing to lose, and only readers to gain. The final big option for self-promotion for science fiction writers is the science fiction convention, but because they are such a part of most writers' professional lives, conventions will be discussed separately later in this chapter.

However, you shouldn't spend large sums of money on promoting your own books. (For one thing, it's unlikely your advance will justify it.) Don't buy ads for yourself—the one exception to that piece of advice would be to take ads in the program book of a convention that is featuring you prominently, but in that case your publisher will often produce and purchase the ad for you if you tell them you'll be attending and ask them to handle it for you. Unless you're really rich, you probably won't be able to afford the kind of advertising that would make a significant difference to your sales. Plus, most authors aren't experienced marketers—we don't know how to put an ad together, or how to read the magazine's specs and requirements. As a rule of thumb, I wouldn't spend much more than postage or the cost of running off a stack of flyers, and then only if you know where you're going to leave them and have something specific to inform people about.

Photos are another expense that tends to be justifiable only later in your career. Until you have several books in print, and regular requests for interviews with photos, there's probably not a lot of point in having expensive photos taken. There's also not a lot of point to photos if your appearance changes drastically on a regular basis—if you change your hair color routinely, or grow and shave facial hair. Photos reflect a stable image, and once you've established that, you won't want to stray too far from it. However, once you do reach that point, a good photo is worth the money it costs to have it done. Look for photographers who are used to helping their subjects create an image—head shot photographers, people who do publicity shots for rock bands, art photographers—rather than pure portrait photographers, unless you have a style and personality that works well with the portrait format. Before you commit to a photo shoot, make sure you've seen the person's work, and generally like what he or she does. Find out in advance how the photographer wants to be credited or what kind of permissions are needed when the photo goes to a magazine. Like photos, outside publicists (i.e., people employed by you rather than by your publisher), tend to be worth their fees only later in your career. However, at that point, they can be very helpful in taking some of the routine work of self-promotion off your hands. In general, though, I wouldn't suggest hiring a publicist unless you have a substantial backlist or a single new and important novel (or better still, both) and that publicist can get you places that neither your publisher nor your agent can reach.

In general, it's important with publicity to know what you want to do, what you're personally able to do, and what results you can reasonably expect. To sell one or two hardbacks (at $22.95 each) at a book signing is actually doing well; the object is less to make money than to make contact with readers. You should probably have some idea of the kind of image your books create. Whether you choose to play with it or against it (like the writer of bloody techno-warfare novels who is actually a placid, soft-spoken teacher of high school physics), it's helpful, in dealing with readers, to have some idea of how they might react.

In general, in science fiction, writers and readers are in much closer contact than in most other genres. Many science fiction writers began as readers—fans—and most science fiction writers (and many readers) spend at least one weekend a year at a science fiction convention. Because of this closeness, many science fiction readers are quite comfortable approaching you, either via mail or e-mail or in person at signings or conventions. Sometimes they're a little too comfortable. I have had people tell me that they expected me to be taller, that they never read books by women but like my work, and that *they* would have written my most recent novel differently, with details—all things that I didn't need to know, and that they would not normally say to someone who they felt was a stranger. Most of the time, though, readers are intelligent and genuinely interested in you and your work. It's important that you treat your readers—any readers—with courtesy and respect. On the most basic level, if you're rude to someone, how likely is it that they'll buy your next book? If they tell their friends that you were obnoxious to them, how many of the friends will buy your next book? You have to be a true genius to get away with really bad behavior, and even then, well, you were still rude.

Science fiction conventions are the main point of contact between writers and readers of SF. According to one source, there is a science fiction convention, large or small, somewhere in the United States every weekend of every year; this schedule includes one- or two-hundred-person specialty conventions, like the ones devoted to Marion Zimmer Bradley's Darkover novels, thousand-person regional conventions, and the six- to seven-thousand-person World Science Fiction Convention, which moves to a different city every year. At nearly every convention, except obviously the ones based on media rather than written SF, writers are very much in evidence. They participate in panel discussions, read from their work, chair roundtable discussions of favorite subjects, hang out with each other, and talk to their fans. Conventions are generally a lot of fun, and worth attending, if only to have a chance to spend some time with other people who like the same thing you do.

However, as a writer, you can expect a few things from conventions. If you were invited to participate, the invitation should have spelled out what you get from the committee (and if it doesn't, you should get that information, in writing, before you agree to come). Generally, any panel participant who isn't the guest of honor can expect a free membership to the convention, and that's about it. You might get a free drink ticket for any convention-wide parties that are held, or be able to cadge free food in the "green room" set up for panelists. A few "cons" still offer a guest membership along with the participant's membership, usually intended for the writer's spouse/partner, but the practice is, sadly, dying out. WorldCon, on the other hand, doesn't even offer free memberships; instead, participants buy their memberships (often at a slightly reduced rate) and are reimbursed once the convention organizers are sure they've made back their expenditures. You're responsible for your own transportation, meals, and hotel room—expenses you may not choose to undertake except for special events. The guests of honor, on the other hand, are usually provided with memberships, free hotel rooms, and transportation. Some cons also provide meals or a meal allowance, some offer spouse memberships or other extras; so, as with all conventions, get the details in writing. If you have any doubts, get your plane ticket (or other transportation money) up front. I've never heard of any convention that deliberately stiffed a guest, but a few conventions, usually new ones run by inexperienced committees, have miscalculated their ability to provide what they promised.

In exchange for this, you're expected to participate in a certain number of panels (the exact number depends on the size of the convention) and to be available to readers. Most convention committees (concoms) will take the time to find out what panels you would like to be on, and to arrange your schedule so that you're not unreasonably overworked, or scheduled during times when you need to be doing something else (like sleeping). If a concom treats you badly, there's not much you can do about it at the convention itself except to walk out—and that may be the right thing to do, if you've been really badly handled. If it's not that bad, check with your fellow pros to see if it's an oversight or a general pattern, and then don't go back to a convention that has mistreated you.

Obviously, SF writers don't go to conventions to make money. Most of us go for two reasons: first, conventions are the most cost-effective ways to promote our books, and, second, they offer an excellent opportunity to meet and spend time with other writers. Most of us don't actually live near that many other people who write SF—or who read it, for that matter—and we carry on most of our contacts and conversations with the SF community at a distance, via mail, e-mail, or phone. Spending real-world time with other people who are doing the same weird job can be very restorative.

The promotional aspect of conventions is very real. I've been told repeatedly, especially when I was starting out, that someone asking for an autograph hadn't read the book, or anything else of mine, but had heard me on a panel and thought my books would be interesting. Because people are judging you and your work on your public persona, you need to take care to be on your best behavior, or better. Always be polite, even when the person you're dealing with is being impossibly rude—if nothing else, you'll look better by contrast. If you get a list of panel topics before the convention (most concoms do try to send schedules in advance), it's worth your while to give them some thought before you actually show up at the panel. You'll sound more coherent if you've already worked out some of your opinions on the subject. If you're the moderator of a panel, prepare a batch of questions ahead of time. That will help you at least postpone the awful moment when everyone looks to you, and you have nothing to say. If you're a panelist in that situation, and you can think of something to say or ask that contributes to the discussion, do it. Everybody will thank you.

Some conventions expect and try to create controversy on their panels. If you find yourself in that situation, and it's not your style, either you can ask to be put on panels with people you know and can trust to be less aggressive, or you can see if your fellow panelists are willing to agree on some ground rules. If you find yourself on a panel with the kind of writers who enjoy arguments for argument's sake, try not to take things personally, maintain a dignified silence if you don't want to participate, and take names. You can refuse to be on panels with certain people, and you don't have to explain your reasons. If controversy is your style, however, remember that not everyone enjoys an argument as much as you do. Being snide or funny at someone's expense may get a laugh, but it may also lose you readers. Give credit where credit's due—if somebody has a good idea, or makes a good point, acknowledge it. Try to keep personalities out of debate as much as possible; if you're using a story as an example of something done well, try to cite the author and title in full so that people can find the book later. If you're giving a negative example, however, it's often more tactful to blur those details, especially if that author is present at the convention.

In general, you're likely to find your fellow writers surprisingly supportive and friendly. A few old-school curmudgeons consider all other writers to be dangerous competition, but that attitude is rare and getting rarer. Most SF writers recognize that we're all in the same difficult and not always rewarding profession, and do what we can to help each other out. If you reach out, ask questions, you're likely to get more advice than you necessarily wanted, from information about publishers and agents to tax issues to matters of craft and art. People you met on a panel, or had long conversations with in the bar one evening, may ask you to join their writing group, or to submit a story to a new anthology they're editing. They may introduce you to their editors, or mention your name when an editor is looking for newer writers. Take the help when you need it, or are offered it: most of the rest of us have been helped out along the way, too. And then, when you get the chance, help someone else get started. According to SF legend, Robert A. Heinlein called this "paying forward." He felt you could never pay anyone back for the help you got; all you could do, he said, was help someone else—pass it along, pay forward.

Writing is often solitary work, performed without a lot of outside help or discussion, and it's important now and then to check in with other people who think what you do is important. Ideally, these people would include your family, but it may not, and, in any case, if your family members aren't also writers, there's a limit to the practical support they can give you. Conventions, where you can meet other writers and establish friendships, are one way to get some of that support. (I have a group of friends, fellow writers whom I see primarily at one convention, which I attend basically to see them.) Another source of support is writers' groups, those weekly or monthly meetings at which a group of writers discuss one of their number's work. Some people find them indispensable; others find them intrusive, more trouble than they're worth. If you do join a group, make sure that the other writers also read and enjoy SF. Otherwise, you may get inappropriate criticism, or blank stares every time you use a term that is conventional to the genre. Also, make sure that you have enough self-confidence to stand up to suggestions that you know are wrong: as I've said before, critics are good at identifying problems, but not nearly as good at offering you solutions. You can achieve some of the same benefits of a writers' group through less formal networking—by keeping in touch with a friend who is also a writer, or exchanging manuscripts with another writer whose work you admire. E-mail facilitates that kind of exchange, and beyond that the Nets are full of writers' discussion groups, some of which are restricted, and some of which anyone can join. They can be very useful, but there's always the hazard that you will find yourself spending more time writing about writing than actually doing it.

After all, the main purpose of all this support is to go on writing. It may be difficult at times—will be, if you want to grow at all as a writer—and one of the reasons to find yourself a support network is to remind yourself of why you wanted to write in the first place. You need to love what you do. Writing isn't generally a lucrative source of income; only a few, exceptional writers reach the income levels associated with the best-sellers. Rather, most of us write because we can make a modest living, or even supplement our day jobs, doing something about which we feel passionately. Even at the worst of times, when nothing goes right, when the prose is clumsy and the ideas feel stale, at least we're doing something that we genuinely love. There's no other reason to work this hard, except that love.

A GLOSSARY OF
SCIENCE FICTION TERMS

My thanks to Don Sakers for the use of his excellent glossary, which makes up the greater part of mine.

AI. A(rtificial) I(ntelligence); SF term for computers that are sophisticated enough to reproduce (or at least mimic) human thought.

Alien. A nonhuman creature, usually intelligent, usually from a world besides Earth. *Aliens* are also referred to as extra-terrestrials (ets) or (affectionately) B.E.M.'s or B(ug)-E(yed) M(onsters).

Alternate History. A world or universe in which history develops along a different path from our own. Perhaps the South won the Civil War, or the dinosaurs never died out, or Mussolini moved to New York in 1935 and opened a trendy East Side deli. Modern physics admits to the possibility of an infinity of *Alternate Histories* and modern SF has taken to the notion. Generally, in an *Alternate History*, natural laws and fundamental physical constraints are the same as in the *Real-World*. See *Dimension(s)*, *Real-World*, *Alternate World(s)*.

Alternate World(s). Usually refers to the present day of an *Alternate History* (q.v.). Also known as *Parallel World(s)*. See *Dimensions*, *Real-World*.

Android. A robot (or, increasingly, a genetic construct) created in the form of a human being. The best *Androids* retain robot abilities such as strength, intelligence, etc., but are outwardly indistinguishable from true humans. (The term "droid," popularized by the Star Wars movies, is clearly derived from *Android* but refers to any robot.)

Anthology. A book of short fiction by many different writers. A *Reprint Anthology* contains material that has already been published, usually in magazines; an original anthology contains stories written specifically for the *Anthology*. See *Collection*.

Collaboration. Story written by a pair (or, more rarely, a trio) of writers. Usually both (or all three) writers have creative control. (A relatively new wrinkle is the collaboration between two writers, one living and one dead.) See *Shared World*, *Franchised World*.

Collection. Book of short fiction by one writer. See *Anthology*.

Con(s). From *convention*. *Real-World* weekend gatherings of SF fans and writers. They range in size from local gatherings of 100+ up to the annual World SF Convention ("WorldCon") at 5,000–7,000. *Cons* exist in every location and for every reason; every weekend of the year sees several *Cons* scheduled in the U.S. and throughout the world. See *Fandom*.

Credit(s). SF term for the generic unit of money; i.e., dinner at a fine restaurant might set you back 25 *Credits*.

Cyberpunk. Subgenre of SF dealing with the *The Net(s)* and its social consequences, usually in a decaying, dystopian urban setting; also those who write in that genre. In its narrowest sense, only writers whose stories appeared in the Anthology *Mirrorshades* can claim to be cyberpunks. However, most SF readers apply the term more loosely to include any work dealing with *The Nets*, virtual reality, direct-to-brain computer interfaces, and/or AI.

Cyberspace. Term coined by SF writer William Gibson to describe the common electronic "space" of *The Net(s)* (q.v.), especially as perceived through virtual reality and direct brain-to-machine connections. In *Cyberspace*, net jockeys use decks (specialized computers) to plug in or jack in (connect their brains directly) to *The Net*.

Dimension(s). A world or universe in which natural laws and/or fundamental physical constants are different from those in the *Real-World*. Sometimes called *Alternate World(s)* (q.v.), although under current usage that term describes something different. In general, *Alternate Worlds* are more similar to the *Real-World* than are other *Dimensions*.

Fandom, Fannish. The worldwide, loose, chaotic subculture of SF and *Fantasy* fans. *Fandom* has its own specialized terminology, its own customs, and its own mindset. In some ways, *Fandom* has the elements of a religion, a political party, a persecuted minority, and a functioning society. The adjective form is *Fannish*. See *Con(s)*, *The Net(s)*.

Fantasy. That branch of literature that generally deals with elements from myth, legend, folktales, fairy tales, etc., usually involving magic or magical entities. See *Science Fiction*, or SF.

Franchised World. Stories by a "junior" (i.e., less famous) writer, set against a background invented and controlled by a "senior" (i.e., more famous) writer. The background may be an established *Universe*, or it may be a new one created for the specific *Franchised World* project. Usually the "senior" writer (or his or her estate) has creative control. See *Shared World, Collaboration, Universe.*

FTL. F(aster) T(han) L(ight) travel or communication; see *Hyperspace, Subspace Communication.*

Future History. A common series of background events shared by a group of stories, usually all by the same writer. See *Series, Shared World, Franchised World, Collaboration, Universe.*

Galactic Empire. Any large-scale political system that includes many different planets. Often a literal empire, governed by a hereditary monarchy, but can also be used loosely to refer to any multiplanetary government, regardless of political system. See *Space Opera.*

Hard SF. *Science Fiction* which involves technology, physics, astrophysics, chemistry, and rigorous adherence to the laws of science. The *What If?* is always the center of a *Hard SF* story, and other facets of storytelling, including characterization, may take second place.

Hugo Awards. Awarded annually by vote of SF fans to the best fiction published in the previous year, in each of four length categories. Also awarded to individuals in several categories such as "Best Editor" and "Best Artist." See *Nebula Awards.*

Hyperspace. A *Dimension* which allows FTL travel. A starship enters *Hyperspace* by means of hyperdrive engines or stargate(s), travels to its destination, then reverses the process to reenter normal space.

Kiloparsec. A distance equal to 1,000 *Parsecs,* or 3,260 *Light Years.* Our Galaxy is about 30 *Kiloparsecs* in diameter.

Light Year. A distance equal to about 9,500,000,000,000 kilometers. The nearest stars are typically 5-10 *Light Years* away. See *Parsec, Kiloparsec.*

Mundane. *Fannish* term (from Latin mundus = world): of or pertaining to the *Real-World.* Non-SF/Fantasy readers are referred to as *Mundanes,* and non-SF/Fantasy books and stories are referred to collectively as *Mundane* literature.

Nebula Awards. Awarded annually by vote of SF writers to the best fiction published in the previous year in each of four length categories. See *Hugo Awards.*

Net(s), The. Worldwide (or larger) data/communications network, the ultimate expression of the "Information Superhighway." SF has dealt with the idea of *The Net* as a social force for twenty years or more. Today, much of the *Real-World* business of SF publishing and the social interactions of *Fandom* are conducted on *The Nets*.

Parallel World(s). See *Alternate World(s)*.

Parsec. A distance equal to 3.26 *Light Years*. The nearest stars are typically 1-5 *Parsecs* away. See *Light Year, Kiloparsec*.

Prequel. A story which precedes the events of another (usually previously published) story set in the same *Universe*. Usually (but not always), a *Prequel* deal with the same characters and/or contributes to setting up the narrative of the other story. See *Series*.

Psi, Psionics. (from distortion of "parapsychology") Mental powers such as *Telepathy*, ESP, etc.

Real-World. SF term that describes the here-and-now Earth of today. See *Mundane, Alternate World(s)*.

Science Fiction (SF). That branch of literature that deals with technological change and its impact on people and society. In marketing/publishing, *Science Fiction* is used as a general term for both SF and *Fantasy*. See *Fantasy*.

Sci-Fi. Abbreviation for *Science Fiction* created by Forrest J. Ackerman in the 1940s. Although it still has its adherents, it is used primarily in reference to the sort of SF that appears in B-grade movies and on network television. Generally considered a pejorative term by most SF readers.

Sequel. A story which follows the events of another story. Usually (but not always) a *Sequel* deals with the same characters and continues or elaborates the narrative of the first story. See *Series*.

Series. A number of stories and/or books which are connected in some way. A *Series* may be (1) A continuous narrative that extends across many stories; (2) One or any number of linked *Sequels*, trilogies, tetrologies, *Prequels*, etc.; (3) A number of otherwise unconnected stories set in the same *Universe*; (4) A set of stories that follow the adventures of a single character or group of characters; (5) Any combination of the above.

Stories in a particular *Series* may be ordered in any of a number of ways: (1) By publication (stories are best read in order by publication date); (2) Chronological (stories are best read in order according to the time frame of the particular *Future History* or *Universe*); (3) No particular order (stories jump around in time, and it doesn't matter where the reader starts or finishes); (4) Any combination of the above.

SF. Preferred abbreviation for *Science Fiction*. See *Sci-Fi*.

Shared World. A common background (and sometimes, characters) used in stories by many different writers. Sometimes a *Shared World* is created by a central editor(s), sometimes by a whole team of writers. Usually, all participants have creative control. See *Franchised World, Collaboration, Anthology, Universe.*

Space Opera. SF stories which are grand, melodramatic, and enormous in scale. Often set against a *Galactic Empire* background, and involving spaceship battles, enormously powerful weapons, and (often) alien races. The emphasis in *Space Opera* is on the (usually outsized) characters and their adventures rather than on the *What If?*

Speculative Fiction. A pseudonym for *Science Fiction*, generally considered both upscale and somewhat pretentious, popularized in the 1960s.

Subspace Communication. A generic method of FTL communication that operates like radio. *Subspace Communication* might be instantaneous, or it might involve some time delay. Sometimes referred to as hyperwave or ultrawave.

Telepathy. The ability to read minds, transfer thoughts, or communicate by mind alone, practiced by a person or alien called a Telepath. See *Psionics.*

Teleportation. The process, mechanical or *Psionic*, of moving instantly from one place to another without crossing the distance between them. Star Trek's Transporter is a *Teleportation* system.

Terraforming. SF term coined by SF writer Jack Williamson. The large-scale engineering process of transforming the environment of a hostile planet (i.e., Mars, Venus, or a planet around another star) into a near-duplicate of Earth's environment.

Universe. A common background (past, present, and/or future) shared by a group of stories, usually all by the same writer. A particular writer can (and usually does) write in many different, distinct *Universes.* Sometimes a writer will produce a story that links two previously unconnected *Universes.*

Other terms you may see instead of *Universe* include *background, milieu, framework, world,* and *cycle.*

What If? The core idea on which an SF novel is based.

WORKS CITED

NONFICTION

Beinhart, L. 1996. *How to Write a Mystery*. New York: Ballantine.

Catron, L. 1984. *Writing, Producing, and Selling Your Play*. Englewood Cliffs, NJ: Prentice-Hall.

Fausto-Sterling, A. 1992. *Myths of Gender: Biological Theories About Women and Men*. New York: Basic Books.

Friesner, E. 1991. Panel discussion at Darkover Grand Council Meeting, Timonium, MD.

Gabrels, R. "Fishing with Architecture." In *Guitar for the Practicing Musician*.

Gould, S. J. 1981. *The Mismeasure of Man*. New York: W.W. Norton.

Keating, H. R. F. 1986. *On Writing Crime Fiction*. New York: St. Martin's Press.

Kushner, E. 1994. Panel discussion at Arisia Conference, Boston, MA.

Maass, D. 1996. *The Career Novelist*. Portsmouth, NH: Heinemann.

Rusch, K. K., and D. W. Smith. 1990. *The SFFWA Handbook*. Eugene, OR: Writers Notebook Press.

Shertzer, M. 1986. *The Elements of Grammar*. New York: Macmillan.

Strunk, W., Jr., and E. B. White. 1979. *The Elements of Style*. New York: Macmillan.

Sweet, J. *The Dramatist's Toolkit*. Portsmouth, NH: Heinemann.

Tavris, C. 1992. *The Mismeasure of Woman*. New York: Simon & Schuster.

Whitfield, S. E., and G. Roddenberry. 1968. *The Making of Star Trek*. New York: Ballentine.

SCIENCE FICTION

Anderson, P. 1958/1978. *The Man Who Counts*. New York: Ace.

———. 1966/1976. *The Trouble Twisters*. New York: Berkeley.

Arneson, E. 1993. *Ring of Swords*. New York: Tor.

Asimov, I. 1957. *The Naked Sun*. New York: Fawcett.

Atwood, M. 1985/1991. *The Handmaid's Tale*. New York: Fawcett.

Blish, J. 1970. *Cities in Flight*. New York: Avon.

Bradley, M. Z. 1962–present. Darkover series. New York: DAW.

Brin, D. 1996. *Glory Season*. New York: Bantam.

Bujold, L. M. 1986–present. Vorkosigan Saga series. New York: Baen Books.

Busby, F. M. 1976. *Rissa Kerguelan*. New York: Berkeley.

———. 1980. *Zelde M'Tana*. New York: Dell.

Carver, J. 1994. *Neptune Crossing*. New York: Tor.

———. 1995. *Strange Attractors*. New York: Tor.

———. 1996. *The Infinite Sea*. New York: Tor.

Charnas, S. M. 1974. *Walk to the End of the World*. New York: Berkeley.

———. 1978. *Motherlines*. New York: Berkeley.

———. 1994. *The Furies*. New York: Tor.

Clarke, A. C. 1973. *Rendezvous with Rama*. New York: Del Rey.

Clarke, A. C., and S. Kubrik. 1968. *2001: A Space Odyssey*. New York: New American Library.

Clement, H. 1953/1974. *Mission of Gravity*. New York: Pyramid.

Daley, B. 1984. *Jinx on a Terran Inheritance*. New York: Del Rey.

———. 1985. *Requiem for a Ruler of Worlds*. New York: Del Rey.

———. 1986. *Fall of the White Ship Avatar*. New York: Del Rey.

Delany, S. R. 1966/1987. *Babel-17*. New York: Bantam.

———. 1990. *Stars in My Pockets Like Grains of Sand*. New York: Bantam.

Dick, P. K. 1996. *Do Androids Dream of Electric Sheep?* New York: Del Rey.

Dowling, T. 1990. *Rynosseros*. North Adelaide, South Australia: Aphelion.

———. 1992. *Blue Tyson*. North Adelaide, South Australia: Aphelion.

———. 1993. *Twilight Beach*. North Adelaide, South Australia: Aphelion.

Engh, M. J. 1995. *Rainbow Man*. New York: Tor.

Gerrold, D. 1972. *When Harlie Was One*. New York: Ballantine.

Gibson, W. 1984/1995. *Neuromancer*. New York: Ace.

Heinlein, R. A. 1957. *Citizen of the Galaxy*. New York: Ballantine.

———. 1966. *The Moon Is a Harsh Mistress*. New York: Berkeley.

Herbert, F. 1965. *Dune*. New York: Ace.

Kurtz, K. 1970–present. Deryni series. New York: Ballentine/Del Ray.

Le Guin, U. K. 1969/1976. *The Left Hand of Darkness*. New York: Ace.

———. 1976. *The Wind's Twelve Quarters*. New York: Bantam.

———. 1994. *A Fisherman of the Inland Sea*. New York: HarperCollins.

Lethem, J. 1994. *Gun, with Occasional Music*. New York: Harcourt Brace.

McCaffrey, A. 1968–present. Dragonriders of Pern series. New York: Del Rey.

McHugh, M. 1992. *China Mountain Zhang*. New York: Tor.

Niven, L., and J. Pournelle. 1987. *The Mote in God's Eye*. New York: Pocket Books.

Norton, A. 1955. *Sargasso of Space*. New York: Ace.

———. 1956/1973. *Plague Ship*. New York: Ace.

———. 1969. *Postmarked the Stars*. New York: Ace.

Panshin, A. 1968. *Star Well*. New York: Ace.

———. 1969. *Masque World*. New York: Ace.

———. 1968. *The Thurb Revolution*. New York: Ace.

Pollack, R. 1994. *Temporary Agency*. New York: St. Martin's Press.

Renault, M. *Fire from Heaven*.

———. *The Mask of Apollo*.

Robinson, K. S. 1993. *Red Mars*. New York: Bantam.

———. 1995. *Green Mars*. New York: Bantam.

———. 1996. *Blue Mars*. New York: Bantam.

Rosenblum, M. 1994. *The Stone Garden*. New York: Del Rey.

Russ, J. 1975. *The Female Man*. New York: Bantam.

Ryman, G. 1994. *The Child Garden*. New York: Orb.

Scott, M. 1985. *Five-Twelfths of Heaven*. New York: Baen Books.

———. 1986. *Silence in Solitude*. New York: Baen Books.

———. 1987a. *The Empress of Earth*. New York: Baen Books.

———. 1987b. *The Kindly Ones*. New York: Baen Books.

——. 1992. *Dreamships*. New York: Tor.

——. 1993. *Burning Bright*. New York: Tor.

——. 1994. *Trouble and Her Friends*. New York: Tor.

——. 1995. *Shadow Man*. New York: Tor.

——. 1996. *Night Sky Mine*. New York: Tor.

——. 1997. *Dreaming Metal*. New York: Tor.

Scott, M., and L. A. Barnett. 1988. *The Armor of Light*. New York: Baen Books.

——. 1995. *Point of Hopes*. New York: Tor.

Starhawk. 1993. *The Fifth Sacred Thing*. New York: Bantam.

Tiptree, J., Jr. 1985. *Brightness Falls from the Air*. New York: Tor.

Vinge, J. 1991a. *Heaven Chronicles*. New York: Warner Books.

——. 1991b. *The Summer Queen*. New York: Warner Books.

——. 1992. *The Snow Queen*. New York: Popular Library.

Williams, W. J. 1995. *Metropolitan*. New York: HarperCollins.

Zelazny, R. 1970–1992. Amber series. New York: Avon.